THE DEVIL'S HISTORIANS

Joseph Mauméjean, Henri Mauméjean, and Charles Mauméjean, detail, *Execution of St. James*, stained glass, 1941 (Église Saint-Jacques, Montgeron, France). This window, created and installed in Nazi-occupied France, depicts the execution of St. James by King Herod. Local tradition holds that Herod looks like Adolf Hitler; if true, this is a subtle act of artistic resistance. While no records of its creation remain, this interpretation fits with some other Mauméjean Brothers works, such as their depiction of the Holocaust in their window "La Messe de St Grégoire" in Église Saint-Pierre-Saint-Paul d'Ivry-sur-Seine. (Photo by Nhuan Doduc)

THE DEVIL'S HISTORIANS

HOW MODERN EXTREMISTS ABUSE THE MEDIEVAL PAST

AMY S. KAUFMAN
AND PAUL B. STURTEVANT

UNIVERSITY OF TORONTO PRESS
Toronto Buffalo London

© University of Toronto Press 2020
Toronto Buffalo London
utorontopress.com
Printed in Canada

ISBN 978-1-4875-8785-7 (cloth)   ISBN 978-1-4875-8786-4 (EPUB)
ISBN 978-1-4875-8784-0 (paper)   ISBN 978-1-4875-8787-1 (PDF)

LIBRARY AND ARCHIVES CANADA CATALOGUING IN PUBLICATION

Title: The devil's historians : how modern extremists abuse the medieval
   past / Amy S. Kaufman and Paul B. Sturtevant.
Names: Kaufman, Amy S., 1974– author. | Sturtevant, Paul B., author.
Description: Includes bibliographical references and index.
Identifiers: Canadiana (print) 2020017780X | Canadiana (ebook)
   20200177842 | ISBN 9781487587857 (cloth) | ISBN 9781487587840
   (paper) | ISBN 9781487587871 (PDF) | ISBN 9781487587864 (EPUB)
Subjects: LCSH: Radicalism. | LCSH: Middle Ages.
Classification: LCC HN49.R33 K38 2020 | DDC 303.48/4—dc23

We welcome comments and suggestions regarding any aspect of our publications—please feel free to contact us at news@utorontopress.com or visit us at utorontopress.com.

Every effort has been made to contact copyright holders; in the event of an error or omission, please notify the publisher.

University of Toronto Press acknowledges the financial assistance to its publishing program of the Canada Council for the Arts and the Ontario Arts Council, an agency of the Government of Ontario.

 Canada Council
for the Arts
Conseil des Arts
du Canada

 ONTARIO ARTS COUNCIL
CONSEIL DES ARTS DE L'ONTARIO
an Ontario government agency
un organisme du gouvernement de l'Ontario

Funded by the   Financé par le
Government   gouvernement
of Canada   du Canada
 Canada

CONTENTS

ACKNOWLEDGMENTS

We would like to thank Natalie Fingerhut and the team at University of Toronto Press, whose excitement about this book and hard work on it have been a joy at every stage. Thanks also to the anonymous peer reviewers for their comments and advice, which helped make this book as good as it can be.

Our collaboration began at *The Public Medievalist*, a free online magazine started by Paul that features scholars who want to share their work with a broader audience. Together, we launched two series of essays on some of the subjects covered in this book: *Race, Racism and the Middle Ages* and *Gender, Sexism and the Middle Ages*. We'd like to thank the editorial staff at the site for their passion, ingenuity, and persistence: Shiloh Carroll, who often held down the fort while this book was in progress; Kristina Hildebrand, who helped smooth out a passage about the Society for Creative Anachronism; as well as editors and contributors Rob Houghton, Vicki Cooper, Sam Brinton, and Arielle Gingold. Thank you also to the scholars who supported and contributed to the site, including the generous awards from the Medieval Academy of America, The Lone Medievalist, and CARMEN. Additional thanks to those who have written for *The Public Medievalist* and those who have read, subscribed to, and shared it. Visit www.publicmedievalist .com for a wide range of articles by some of Medieval Studies' best scholars if you want to learn more about the Middle Ages or about medievalism in the modern world.

ADDITIONAL ACKNOWLEDGMENTS FROM AMY S. KAUFMAN

My work on this book would not have been possible without Kathleen Coyne Kelly, who first introduced me to medievalism studies, whose own brilliant scholarship has always set the highest bar, and who has been a supportive mentor and friend throughout my career. I'm also deeply grateful to Susan Aronstein, Laurie Finke, Kevin Harty, Don Hoffman, Marty Shichtman, and Elizabeth Sklar, who welcomed me when I was just a baby medievalist and who have inspired and encouraged my work ever since. Thanks to all the scholars at the International Society for the Study of Medievalism whose support, care, and mentoring were invaluable, especially Pam Clements, Karl Fugelso, Carol Robinson, M.J. Toswell, Richard Utz, and Usha Vishnuvajjala. Thanks to Phillip Edward Phillips for the years of encouragement and friendship, and for telling me to ditch the book I didn't care about so I could write the book I wanted to write instead. Middle Tennessee State University provided a 2016 research award that helped fund the early work for this book. Cory Rushton and Usha Vishnuvajjala were my lifelines throughout the writing process—this book would not exist without you either. Finally, thank you to Mike James: for your confidence and support, for the late-night beer runs, and for being the world's best second set of eyes.

ADDITIONAL ACKNOWLEDGMENTS FROM PAUL B. STURTEVANT

DURING THE creation of this book, my mother, Professor Elizabeth G. Sturtevant, died after a long battle with Parkinson's disease and multiple system atrophy. On all levels, both literal and figurative, I would not be the person I am today had it not been for her. I wish she had been able to read this one. I think she would have liked it.

Many of my friends, family, and colleagues were incredibly supportive throughout. Particular thanks to Cash Colburn, Tom Caiazza, Jacky Hart, Lee Braddock, Elizabeth Hickernell, and Kay Oss; you were there at the worst. And last, thank you to my partner Arielle Gingold for helping me to keep putting one foot in front of the other, and for reminding me that sometimes it's okay not to.

INTRODUCTION:
WEAPONIZING HISTORY

> There is no reason, I feel, to object when antiquity draws no
> hard line between the human and the supernatural: it adds
> dignity to the past, and, if any nation deserves the privilege
> of claiming a divine ancestry, that nation is our own.
> —Livy, *History of Rome*, c. 27–25 BCE[1]

D URING ANCIENT Rome's Golden Age, from 27 BCE to 180
CE, Augustus Caesar enacted a series of reforms focused on
regulating Roman family life. He passed what became known
as the Julian marriage laws, which criminalized adultery for
married women. Fathers could kill adulterous daughters, and
husbands who did not divorce cheating wives could be pros-
ecuted. Augustus's laws also encouraged people to produce
more Roman citizens: he gave money to families with three or
more children, and he levied taxes against unmarried Romans.
He also banned women from attending gladiatorial fights and
athletic events to keep them "pure," even exiling his own
daughter and granddaughter for "vice."

Augustus's reforms were meant to take Rome back to
a time that he imagined was simpler, and better. But his
reforms were also reactionary, part of a backlash against
rising female power in Rome. By Augustus's reign, some
women had begun to reject arranged marriages. They could
own property, get divorced, and even participate in politics
in limited ways. Some women gave public speeches, others
agitated to be gladiators. Thus, Augustus's new laws aimed
to limit the threat that women's liberation presented to both
patriarchal and aristocratic power. (After all, when women
are free to choose their sexual partners, family dynasties tend
to fall apart.)

2 / The Devil's Historians

Augustus also argued that women's immodesty jeopardized the Roman state. Fresh from his victory over Mark Antony and Cleopatra, the emperor warned his people that Rome had almost fallen under the influence of a willful woman—and a foreign one, at that. He proposed that in order to restore its greatness, Rome should go back in time, to its simpler, more virtuous, male-dominated past.

Although Augustus lived in ancient Rome, he relied on myths about *even more ancient* Rome for his notions of ideal femininity. He praised the Sabine women who, according to legend, were raped by the first Roman men but stayed with them for the sake of their children. He also touted the bravery of Lucretia, who was raped by the son of a tyrannical king and killed herself in shame, a tragedy that led to the establishment of Rome's Republic. Augustus, in short, wielded Rome's past—or at least, his mythical version of it—as a weapon. He used it to control what the Roman people, especially Roman women, could do with their lives.

The blissful, simpler Rome that Augustus hoped his moral reforms would bring back is not what you or I would consider historical. There was no bold line in the ancient world between myth and fact. As our epigraph suggests, some ancient Romans believed it was more important for history to teach people lessons in the present, or to confirm a nation's illusions about itself, than it was for history to be factually true.

That just goes to show you: there's no story about the past too early, or too implausible, for people to turn it into propaganda.

MISUSING HISTORY

AUGUSTUS IS far from the only person who weaponized "history" to punish and control people. This book will show you many of the ways history has been used to oppress others, spread hatred and fear, and even lead people into war.

And oftentimes, those who use history to incite violence and discrimination misrepresent the past, or sometimes outright lie about it, in order to sway public opinion.

We tend to think of the past as rigid and fixed, simply a collection of things that happened. But *history* isn't the same thing as *the past*. History is our way of rendering the past into stories. Our whole view of an event can shift depending on who becomes the main character of the story, which perspectives we decide to look through, or even which perspectives are available to us. For example, the Bayeux Tapestry—one of the primary narratives of the Norman Conquest—was once considered a relatively unbiased account of William the Conqueror's conquest of England in 1066. But recent historians realized just how skewed the tapestry's perspective actually is when they learned it may have been commissioned by William's half-brother.[2] The Bayeux Tapestry is a perfect visual representation of the old cliché that history is written by the victors.

Even when historical bias isn't quite this obvious, when history is unclear or incomplete, or when we have competing narratives of what happened, people tend to prefer stories that flatter their illusions about themselves or their ancestors. For instance, in Augustus's time, there were at least two competing Roman origin stories. There's the one you probably know, in which the brothers Romulus and Remus—raised by a she-wolf and favored by the god of war—battled to the death for control of the city they founded. But another version was that Rhome, a Trojan woman who fled the destruction of Troy with other survivors, got tired of sailing around and talked everyone into settling in Latinum. The new city was called Rome in her name. Take one guess which founding legend the warlike, patriarchal Roman government decided to promote.

Yet, although history has multiple perspectives, that doesn't mean all we can do is throw up our hands and decide the past is just a matter of opinion. Finding the truth means sifting through all those perspectives to figure out what really happened. And the stories we choose to tell or to omit matter very much in the present. For instance, some people in the United States refer to the American Civil War—some in jest and some in all seriousness—as the "War of Northern Aggression." The name is part of what's known as the Lost Cause account of the Civil War, an attempt to rehabilitate the Confederacy that claims slavery was a benevolent institution and that the Civil War was caused by economic factors, not slavery. The Lost Cause narrative isn't just some fringe conspiracy theory: it made its way into some states' history textbooks and had been, until recently, the dominant narrative in many southern classrooms. And while this may be the way Confederates viewed things during the war, that doesn't make it true.[3] Ignoring the suffering of millions of enslaved Americans doesn't make them disappear.

When we're presented with multiple perspectives on history, we can determine whether someone is misusing the past or wielding history as a weapon not just by checking the facts (although that can be useful), but by examining which stories they choose to tell, the purpose behind their stories, and the effects those stories have in the present day. History has many uses. It helps us understand ourselves and each other. It helps us feel connected to a wider world, and it can give our day-to-day actions meaning. It can even inspire us to fight injustice. But when histories are rewritten or ignored, when common misunderstandings are manipulated, or when the past is used to promote prejudice, oppression, and complacency in the face of injustice, these are misuses.

As we illustrate in the following pages, the misuse of the past is rarely innocent. Far from being just "another version" of a story, the misuse of history can get people killed.

THE DANGERS OF "HISTORY"

T HE WEAPONIZATION of history doesn't always involve actual facts about the past. It can rely on a foggy perception of history: a general, impressionistic sense of how things were, or even how they always have been. Sometimes it relies on what we now consider myth and legend. But accuracy does not always matter to people who are so attached to their ideas about the past that those myths are part of their identity.

Murky historical narratives can offer toxic ideologies a patina of tradition or timelessness that make them seem natural, correct, or inevitable. And once that occurs, misconceptions can be difficult to shift. That's why misuses of the past are so important to recognize and rectify. For instance, resistance to tearing down Confederate statues in American cities comes from the myth that the statues are politically neutral, merely a way to remember a war and honor the dead. But the truth is, most of these statues were erected in the twentieth century by groups with explicitly white supremacist agendas—like the United Daughters of the Confederacy, who promoted the Lost Cause narrative and even built a monument to the Ku Klux Klan. As the mayor of New Orleans, Mitch Landrieu, said in a speech on 19 May 2017 about the decision to tear down his city's confederate monuments:

> These statues are not just stone and metal. They are not just innocent remembrances of a benign history. These monuments purposefully celebrate a fictional, sanitized Confederacy; ignoring the death, ignoring the enslavement, and the terror that it actually stood for.[4]

Augustus's narrative of a simpler, better Rome "back then" conflated foggy history with myth and legend, and he wasn't the only historical personage who misused the imagined past to fuel his imperialistic goals. The English used the myth that they were descended from King Arthur (who probably didn't exist, or if he existed, may only have been a general)[5] to justify waging war on the world: enslaving Africans, colonizing India, and murdering Native Americans, First Nations, and other Indigenous peoples. Germany followed a similar path of myth-propelled destruction in World War II. The fantasy of the "Aryan race," created by German historians and folklorists, held that white Germans were descended from a group of prehistoric Indo-Europeans who created all of humanity's religious and cultural achievements (including those in India and ancient Greece). This was easily proven false, but that hardly mattered. Nazi propaganda weaponized the historical myth of Aryan superiority to attack its neighbors and commit one of the worst atrocities in human history, the Holocaust. In fact, if you look at any murderous regime, odds are good that it is using a warped version of history to justify its crimes.

THE MOST MISUNDERSTOOD HISTORY OF ALL

If HISTORY has always been misused, why are we focusing on the Middle Ages specifically? To some degree, that's because this is our specialty. But the medieval period is also particularly murky in the modern imagination. It is one of the most popular—and one of the most deeply misunderstood—eras in world history. It's the historical moment that people either love to love, or love to hate. And as violent, authoritarian regimes rise up around the world, medieval "history" is making an unfortunate comeback. From the neo-caliphate of the Islamic State (also known as ISIS, ISIL, or Daesh) to white supremacist terrorists with crusader slogans in their manifestos and on their guns, myths about the Middle Ages are being forged into weapons that threaten everyone in the twenty-first century.

Modern people have strange ideas about the so-called Dark Ages. Many of these ideas come from both popular culture and a long history of dismissive scholarship. People imagine that medieval life was filthy, backwards, and rife with random acts of murder and torture; that medieval men were "real" men and that medieval women were utterly powerless; that everyone was a religious zealot and that faith and superstition governed every aspect of daily life. These sweeping generalizations make the Middle Ages less a historical past and more a mythological past. The fact that many fictional worlds are set in someone's idea of the Middle Ages both illustrates the problem and contributes to it.

Today's medievalist scholars will jump at the chance to tell you that there is no such thing as the "Dark Ages."[6] The myth of a supposedly ignorant set of centuries taking up space between the bright, glorious ancient world and the sparkling intellect of the Renaissance is a wildly inaccurate image of the past that distorts hundreds of years of human history. But like the other myths we have mentioned so far, it is a hard story to kill because it makes people feel better about themselves. "I'm so glad I didn't live back then," we tell each other, or we might say, "that idea is *practically medieval....*" when we want to feel smarter than someone else. And because we believe the Middle Ages were simpler times, with simpler people, they are a landscape we like to imagine ourselves conquering—whether in comical stories about modern people tumbling into the medieval past, like Mark Twain's *A Connecticut Yankee in King Arthur's Court*, or as avatars in the digital world swinging swords and winning castles of our own.

On the other hand, people who are disenchanted with the innovations of modern society often idealize the Middle Ages as natural and pure, the "original" condition of humankind. These people see the Middle Ages as a landscape for heroism, passion, and legendary deeds. When emerging industrial capitalism created new heights of human misery in the nineteenth century, the Middle Ages came back into vogue as an idyllic, rural counterpoint. The Middle Ages have also been wielded as a weapon when traditional power structures are threatened: in Victorian England, when so many colonized peoples struggled to free themselves from British rule, during Reconstruction in the United States, and throughout the movement for women's suffrage on both sides of the pond. The fantasy of a pure, orderly patriarchal and monarchical medieval past in which everyone knew his or her place gives people the "historical" evidence they think they need to resist social progress. Using the Middle Ages this way is not just wrong, it is also *wrong*. By that, we mean it's not just morally reprehensible—it's also historically inaccurate.

With this book, we hope to expose and challenge the many dangerous fantasies—past and present—that are based on misperceptions of medieval history. We do this not because we want to ruin people's fantasies, and not because we feel the Middle Ages is some sacred, pure space that needs to be protected, but because myths about the Middle Ages have a long and terrible legacy of being used to hurt people. Medieval history is too often wielded by the powerful to justify their opposition to positive changes in the world, or to feed their prejudices about people they deem inferior. As medievalists, we are passionate about challenging these uses of the Middle Ages whenever and wherever we find them, and equally passionate about helping people explore the real history of a diverse, rich, and complex medieval world.

Whether you are reading this book in your history class or in your favorite armchair, we hope it will give you a clearer vision of the medieval past and make it easier for you to separate fact from fiction. Because the Middle Ages are not going away anytime soon. History is too powerful a rhetorical tool for people with violent agendas to ignore it. But hopefully, after reading this book, you'll be better equipped to disarm their propaganda.

1

THE MIDDLE AGES: FOUNDATIONAL MYTHS

> The Middle Ages are at the root of all our contemporary
> "hot" problems, and it is not surprising that we go back to
> that period every time we ask ourselves about our origin.
> —Umberto Eco, "The Return of the Middle Ages," 1986[1]

POPULAR CULTURE sends a lot of mixed messages about the Middle Ages. Some books, movies, and video games represent it as an era of heroic knights and epic battles, while others portray the medieval past as a dark, dangerous time when anyone who stepped out of line would be burned as a witch. Despite these dramatic differences, there are a few things contemporary people consider "common knowledge" about the Middle Ages: that medieval lives were nasty, brutish, and short; that this part of the past was a white, Christian man's world; and that medieval people were so religious and superstitious that they would throw their neighbor on the pyre for using her broom a little too often.

The problem is, common knowledge is wrong.

Take the witch trials, for instance. They're considered a medieval phenomenon, but they were far more prevalent during the Renaissance, when they became official legal practice. The Church didn't even officially recognize the existence of witches until the end of the Middle Ages, around 1484. The witch trials took off when a treatise called the *Malleus Maleficarum*—which translates into English as *The Hammer of Witches*—was published in 1487. Written by former Inquisitor Heinrich Kramer (who was fired from the Inquisition for being overzealous, if you can imagine that), the *Malleus Maleficarum* taught people how to identify and torture witches and advocated for their execution.

Thanks in part to the invention of the moveable-type printing press, which significantly sped up the transmission of texts and ideas in Europe, the *Malleus Maleficarum* grew wildly popular after Kramer's death. Rampant, violent persecutions of accused witches spread across Europe and the colonies. This lasted for centuries (including, famously, the Salem witch trials). The 1600s, the height of the Renaissance, saw mass executions of suspected witches. Hundreds of people were murdered in a single German city.[2]

Why does it matter if people think the witch trials were a few centuries earlier than they actually occurred? It may seem harmless when people get history wrong like this, but it can be dangerous too. If we believe witch trials are one of the defining features of the Middle Ages, we can imagine that "civilized" cultures left torture and religious persecution behind in the Dark Ages. We can pretend that torture was a phenomenon cured by science and the Enlightenment—completely ignoring the torture and executions still going on today, such as the "enhanced interrogation" practiced by the United States.

INVENTING THE PAST

WHY DO medieval people have such terrible reputations? How did the Middle Ages become the dumping ground for all of humanity's bad behavior? This view of medieval people has been with us since the Middle Ages were invented. And, yes, the Middle Ages were invented.

Italian humanists in the fifteenth century were the first to describe history in the three-part system (ancient, medieval, and modern) we know today. Leonardo Bruni called 476–1250 CE a "middle period" in his 1442 *History of the Florentine People*;[3] Flavio Biondo chose the dates 410–1400 CE in his 1483 *Decades of History from the Deterioration of the Roman Empire*.[4] Giovanni Bussi preferred the more poetic *media tempestas*—"middle season" in the 1469 preface to his edition of the works of Roman writer Apuleius.[5] Clear in each of these designations is the sense that the years we know as the "Middle Ages" are *in between* two more important, more monumental eras. Renaissance humanists considered the medieval past an interruption between their own enlightened time and the classical Greek and Roman eras they revered.

Thanks to the preservation and translation of ancient Greek and Roman texts by medieval Jewish, Muslim, and Byzantine scholars—and thanks in part to the printing press—Europe in the fifteenth and sixteenth centuries gained increased access to classical philosophy, art, literature, science, and history. Inspired to draw on the wisdom of ancient Greece and Rome to enrich their own cultures, scholars began to call the period between the classical world and their world a "Dark Age." Thus, the Middle Ages were born out of resentment, seen as the centuries that broke Europe's connection to a glorious, ancient past. With the stroke of a few quills, the lives, experiences, and accomplishments of millions of people over hundreds of years were consigned to the trash heap of history, and the idea of the Middle Ages as the Dark Ages has been with us ever since.

Most scholars today don't use the term *Dark Ages*, thanks to being corrected by generations of angry medievalists. But the concept persists, in part, because the idea of a time so much worse than our own allows us to feel superior. In fact, myths about the Middle Ages are so persistent that scholars have developed methods for thinking, and talking, about the way the medieval period is used and abused. We use the term *medievalism* to describe the way filmmakers, game designers, artists, musicians, and even everyday people at your local Renaissance faire imagine the Middle Ages.

Life in the twenty-first century can make the medieval world seem very far away, but we still live in a world full of popular medievalisms: video games franchises like *Crusader Kings*, *Dragon Age*, *The Witcher*, and *The Elder Scrolls*; never-ending movie adaptations of King Arthur and Robin Hood; and wildly popular television shows like *Vikings* and *Game of Thrones*. Weekend warriors don handmade medieval outfits for historical reenactments or cosplay, and writers keep spinning out medieval-themed fantasy novels for your Kindle. You could spend a lifetime playing in the Middle Ages without once setting foot in a museum or on a historical site.

As widespread and varied as it is, medievalism also tends to court historical inaccuracies. And these aren't just meaningless errors. They can tell us a lot about ourselves. Italian philosopher and writer Umberto Eco wrote that "the Middle Ages have always been messed up in order to meet the vital requirements of different periods."[6] In other words, how we imagine the past—and the way we *mis*remember it—can be a window into the present. Our view of the past reveals our understanding of the world, our highest hopes and our darkest fears.

What people get wrong about the Middle Ages, and why they do it, are questions we hope to answer in this book. But first, in this chapter, we'll debunk some of the most common misunderstandings of the medieval world. And as you'll see in the rest of the book, these misconceptions are far from harmless. They fuel some of the most dangerous movements in the world today.

MYTH: MEDIEVAL PEOPLE'S LIVES WERE NASTY, BRUTISH, AND SHORT

IT'S HARD to find a version of the Middle Ages in popular culture where the knights aren't rusty brutes, the peasants aren't covered in mud, and the landscape isn't ravaged by war. Just turn on Netflix or HBO. Life in the Middle Ages just seems harder: plagues swept the world, dramatic climate change led to food shortages, unstable political power created unpredictable violence, religious prejudice and superstitions were common, and no one had invented a single iPhone. Terrible. But the truth is, the medieval period wasn't radically different from other historical eras. You'll often hear facts thrown around like, "Medieval people only lived to be 35!" But claims like this fall apart upon closer examination. Life expectancy is an average, and it includes infant mortality. While many more infants and children died in the Middle Ages (and throughout all historical periods until modern medicine), the average person who survived the vulnerable years of childhood lived to be in their 70s, just as they do today. And, just like today, wealth and access to health care tended to be determining factors.

The medieval period is also considered a uniquely violent era, and it's easy to assume that widespread war—the Hundred Years' War, the Mongol invasions, the early Muslim conquests, the Crusades—cut most medieval people's lives short. But war is one of the horrifying constants of human history. It is not uniquely medieval. And while the hand-to-hand combat that is the hallmark of much of medieval warfare may feel more brutal and savage than, say, a drone strike, the murderous capability of the latter far outstrips the former. The Geneva conventions outlawed the intentional targeting of civilians in war, but they were enacted in 1949, after the worst civilian massacres in history: the bombings of Dresden, Tokyo, Hiroshima, and Nagasaki. None of the death tolls in any medieval battle can compare to these tragedies.

The medieval plague seems to stand out as a particularly horrific historical phenomenon, in part because it seized the imagination of one of the medieval world's most famous writers: Giovanni Boccaccio, whose *Decameron*, a collection of short tales told by noble characters quarantined during the Black Death, was so popular that his stories were translated and adapted by Chaucer, Shakespeare, Tennyson, Keats, and even contemporary filmmakers like Pier Paolo Pasolini and Jeff Baena.[7] But most of humanity—not just medieval people—lacked the ability to fight infections or even understand how they spread for much of history. England during the Renaissance suffered regular deadly outbreaks of plague, smallpox, syphilis, typhus, malaria, and a mysterious illness called "sweating sickness." Upon contact with Europeans, upwards of 95 per cent of the Indigenous peoples of the Americas were killed by European diseases. Plagues even ravaged the twentieth century: from 1918–1920, half a *billion* people were infected with the Spanish Flu global pandemic, which killed between 50 and 100 million people. And let's not forget that we are currently living with the global pandemic of HIV/AIDS.

Medieval people's supposed ignorance and filth is blamed for these waves of disease. *Monty Python and the Quest for the Holy Grail* and "gritty" television dramas like *Game of Thrones* teach us that medieval people were constantly covered in muck. But real medieval people enjoyed bathing regularly, especially medieval Vikings. English chroniclers remarked on the Vikings' cleanliness and suave attire, and worried that they would seduce all the English women because of it. Soap—which medieval people made and used regularly (there were entire guilds of soapmakers)—would not have saved anyone from the Black Death. Only penicillin would. For that, humanity would have to wait until 1928.

The myth that medieval people lived horrible, short lives persists because we believe that we are more advanced, more sophisticated, more civilized, and frankly, better than the people who have come before us. But this historical chauvinism easily slips into racism and xenophobia when it is applied to the modern world. People often use the word *medieval* to describe the developing world, or accuse the people in these countries of being "stuck in the Dark Ages," suggesting that they are "backwards," uneducated, or unusually violent. In these cases, "medieval" is almost always a racist insult hurled by inhabitants of majority-white nations who believe their own culture is superior. Politicians and pundits will also use the word *medieval* to refer to anything they want to portray as backwards, barbaric, or stupid. This allows their audiences to think they are better than those terrible medieval people: torture is "medieval torture," despite the fact that your own country might practice it. Rape is "medieval," despite the modern world having globalized the practice of human trafficking.[8]

You can see this kind of rhetoric in the wars waged in Afghanistan, Iraq, Yemen, and Syria, and in anti-immigration rhetoric flung around the United States and Europe.[9] Calling something modern "medieval" is a rejection, and can cause us to mock people's pain, dismiss their deaths, invade their countries to "liberate" them, and lock them up when they cross international borders or ask for refuge. In short, calling people "medieval" suggests that they—along with historical medieval people—are less human than we are.

MYTH: MEDIEVAL PEOPLE WERE UNEDUCATED, ILLITERATE, AND IGNORANT

WHEN PUBLIC figures want to accuse each other of being ignorant or authoritarian, they say their opponent is "from the Dark Ages" or "practically medieval." But why do we believe that medieval people's intellectual capacity was so radically different from our own? Part of the problem is the outsized assessment of just how much the world changed in the Renaissance.

It's quite clear that *something* big happened in Europe over the course of the fifteenth and sixteenth centuries. In fact, several big things did. Around 1439, Johannes Gutenberg introduced the moveable-type printing press to Europe, giving average people access to books that had previously been available only to scholars or the wealthy. In the late 1400s, European explorers sailed to Africa and the Americas, setting out on a program of slavery, genocide, and destruction that would turn European nation-states into maritime empires. And in 1517, a German monk named Martin Luther published his *Ninety-Five Theses* (though he probably did not nail them to any doors) and launched the Protestant Reformation.

Each of these events is used to mark the moment of European modernity, the spark of intellectual and national growth that separated the Middle Ages from what came afterwards. These discoveries supposedly allowed Europe to advance out of the "Dark Ages" and move into the light. But before we talk about the intellectual accomplishments of the Middle Ages—which, contrary to popular opinion, had a light of their own—it's important to note the darkness that followed some of modernity's most noted developments.

The Protestant Reformation, for instance, may have resulted in a more accessible faith, but it was also a violent and destructive revolution. People were executed over minor theological disagreements like the doctrine of transubstantiation, monasteries were raided and burned, churches were whitewashed, wiping centuries-old art off their walls, and sculptures and artifacts were smashed in systematic raids—not unlike the path of historical devastation ISIS waged against art and architecture in the Middle East. Moreover, the Renaissance saw the beginning of colonialism and the transatlantic slave trade. Explorers like Christopher Columbus devastated and enslaved whole populations in search of plunder, not to prove anyone wrong about the earth being flat.

By the way, the flat-earth story promoted by Columbus fans is a flat-out lie. And more than that: it's a lie that shows just how dependent our modern sense of self is on the myth of an ignorant past. Medieval people were well aware that the earth is round. Medieval Muslim scholars, for example, knew the earth was spherical and developed trigonometry to measure its geography and determine their distance from, and direction to, Mecca. Medieval Christian scholars knew the earth was round too: thirteenth-century astronomer Johannes de Sacrobosco wrote a treatise called *De Sphaera Mundi*—Latin for *On the Sphere of the World*—that discussed the spherical nature of the earth in its first chapter. And this wasn't some sort of academic secret. Popular medieval writers like the author of *Mandeville's Travels* casually referenced the round earth. Columbus did not sail west because he believed the world was round when others thought it flat—he did so under the misguided belief that the world was much smaller than astronomers had calculated. This is why he thought he had landed in India rather than on another continent. Columbus wasn't a maverick. He simply didn't trust the experts.

In fact, apart from a few flat-earth conspiracy theorists over the years, people have known the earth is round since ancient times, all the way back to Aristotle. And that brings us to another point about the intellectual culture of medieval Europe: although many more classical texts flooded Europe during the Renaissance, medieval people had access to classical literature and philosophy too, thanks in part to the efforts of medieval Muslim and Jewish scholars and translators. These translations ushered in what is known as the Twelfth-Century Renaissance, a period of flourishing art, literature, science, and philosophy in medieval Europe, and one of many "mini-renaissances" that happened thanks to intercultural exchange.

Medieval people were just as intellectual, just as curious about the world, and just as adept at complex mental tasks as you are (and that's not an insult). Just because they did not have some of the same technological or cultural developments at their fingertips did not change their interest in, or capacity for, learning. For example, many of the intellectual pillars of society that we enjoy today were invented during the Middle Ages, like universities, which have been around since at least the ninth century. The University of al-Qarawiyyin, in Fez, Morocco, was established by Fatima al-Fihri in 859 CE. Europe saw its first universities in the eleventh century in Bologna, Paris, and Oxford. And while these universities were often centers of theological education, contrary to popular belief, medieval scholars did not spend their time contemplating the number of angels that could fit on the head of a pin. Medieval universities were dedicated to teaching law, medicine, and the arts in addition to theology, and cultivated some of the greatest minds of the Middle Ages.

And yes, the Middle Ages did produce some truly staggering intellects, like Ibn Sina (also known as Avicenna), an eleventh-century Persian polymath who developed systems of formal logic and scientific inquiry, and whose works *The Book of Healing* and *The Canon of Medicine* became the standard texts for nearly 500 years. Medieval medicine was far more involved than leeches, magic, and prayer. Medieval doctors developed chemical processes for the distillation of medicines and intricate surgical procedures as difficult as removing gallstones and cataracts. Albertus Magnus, a thirteenth-century philosopher whose writing brought

Aristotle's ideas back into medieval Europe, developed scientific treatises on logic, astronomy, minerology, physiology, law, morality, and geography. And women participated in medieval intellectual culture too, like Hildegard of Bingen, whose twelfth-century medical and theological texts influenced generations of scholars.

These institutional and textual methods of sharing knowledge were not the only education medieval people had. Myths about uneducated medieval people tend to privilege written wisdom over other means of transmitting information. Some medieval peasants may not have been literate, but that didn't make them fools. People have always shared information, discoveries, and history orally. This includes knowledge of stories, song, art, architecture, medicine, and even agricultural and cooking techniques. The fetish for the written word as the height of knowledge is part of what led Western scholars to ignore the history of cultures other than Greece and Rome for centuries, and it's also partly to blame for the bizarre modern racist conspiracy theory that ancient cultural achievements were secretly built by aliens. It is hardly good historical practice to dismiss entire groups of people just because they could not read.

MYTH: MEDIEVAL PEOPLE HAD NO INDIVIDUALITY

IF YOU'VE ever watched a movie about the Middle Ages, you might believe the medieval period was an era of all-powerful kings and nobles who ruled with iron fists. And don't get us started on popular perceptions of the medieval Church, which is usually imagined as a cross between a dystopian surveillance state and the mafia. Political and religious power was far more diffuse and diverse in the Middle Ages than popular culture would have you believe. For one thing, the "divine right of kings"—a theory that kings ruled with direct approval from God, and thus were not subject to contradiction by popes or parliaments—was a post-medieval phenomenon. It wasn't until after the Middle Ages that European kings consolidated legislative, judicial, and executive power into their own person; *they* were the tyrants who could (and did) have people executed on a whim. Medieval rulers were far less powerful. Despite what various iterations of the Robin Hood legend might tell you, they did not collect revenues simply by shaking down peasants. In Norman England, the king's income came from rents on the lands he personally held, the obligations owed to him by the lords and knights who swore fealty to him, income from tolls and fines, and property taxes. But even these taxes were notoriously easy to avoid and collected inconsistently—wealthy people dodging taxes has an unsurprisingly long history.

A medieval king's power was often limited, and managing a kingdom could be an exercise in herding ambitious, heavily armed cats. Medieval chronicles are filled with examples of knights and lords ignoring royal dictates, or even pledging their loyalty to more than one ruler, which caused difficulties when these rulers went to war with each other. For example, the fourteenth-century *Chronicle of Hainaut* tells the story of Jacques of Avenses, a knight who found a way to game the system by pledging loyalty to several different local lords, then collecting castles from most of the landowners in the region. Each of these lords eventually got fed up with Jacques and had to spend considerable time and resources going to war with him to get their castles back.

Some medieval people were not ruled by monarchs at all. Take Iceland, for example. From its foundation in the tenth century until it fell under the dominion of the King of Norway in 1262, Iceland was ruled by what was called an *Alþing*. The *Alþing* was a general assembly of sorts, where a group of the land's most powerful and wealthy leaders gathered to make laws and decide legal questions. While not a democracy exactly (it is best understood as a type of oligarchy—rule by a small group of privileged people), it had democratic elements: all free men were permitted to attend the *Alþing* and plead their cases, and the rulers (called the *goðar*) were influenced by the popular opinions of their friends and neighbors. Even after Iceland became a subject of Norway in the thirteenth century, the Norwegian king's power was limited on the island. The *Alþing* continued, but became a coequal legislative branch of government.

England did have kings before the Norman Conquest in 1066, but it also had a system of government that prioritized local power over state power. The English developed law by committee, first in the village *moot* (meeting); then in a *hundred moot* with nearby villages, presided over by a thane; then by a *shire moot* presided over by an earl or his representative; and then by the *witana gemoot*, a parliament that advised the king. The medieval Italian peninsula had a wide range of independent city-states that were run as republics. Even the Holy Roman Empire was never actually an empire, but instead a complex confederacy of smaller kingdoms, principalities, duchies, counties, free cities, theocratic prince-bishoprics, and random patches of land ruled in other ways. Its emperor was actually *elected* by a council of the highest-ranking noblemen.

The Middle Ages featured as much diversity in political systems and leadership as any other historical period. Many historians nowadays question whether the term *feudalism* is even useful, because in reality, there was not one "feudal system" to which everyone ascribed, but instead a patchwork of agreements among powerful people based as much on local custom and tradition as adherence to some larger ideal.

But what about religion? you might be thinking. *Surely every medieval person was told what to think by the Catholic Church?* On the contrary, religious diversity was a predominant feature of the Middle Ages. First of all, the Middle Ages were not only limited to western Europe. Scholars disagree on where the geographical boundaries of the Middle Ages are (or if there indeed are any such boundaries),[10] but suffice it to say that medieval studies have regularly included areas like modern-day Greece, Turkey, and the Middle East, North Africa, Sicily, Spain, the Balkans and Scandinavia—and the scope broadens every year. Each of these areas had significant populations of Muslims, Orthodox and Coptic Christians, Jews, Hindus, and people of other faiths. But even if we limit ourselves to looking only at Catholic-dominated Europe, not only were communities of Jews living alongside the Christians, there were significant differences in religious beliefs and practices even within the same faith.

Medieval Christians expressed a range of relationships and attitudes toward the Church. Theologians like Marguerite Porete rebelliously wrote that God is love and was burned at the stake for it. Chaucer's *Canterbury Tales* are full of corrupt, sexually rapacious monks and friars alongside a devout, morally pure parson. The Robin Hood ballads feature a hero who chops the heads off of monks after he prays to the Virgin Mary. Iceland had been converted to Christianity by the time the sagas were written down, but many Norse poems, like the Eddas, record the exploits of the Norse gods, not the Christian one. Moreover, for some people, religion may have entailed a set of cultural practices more than an expression of personal zeal. For Christian writers like Dante and William Langland, faith is the topic of the text. Muslim and Jewish writers brilliantly blended the religious and secular to produce some of the world's most beautiful poetry. But for other writers, religion is either an incidental part of the background or is absent entirely.

Despite all this, even scholars have been slow to recognize medieval people's individuality. Up until recently, many history books would tell you that medieval society was fundamentally different from our own: more collectivist and less liberated.[11] Medieval people, we were told, did not think of themselves as individuals, but as part of family or social groups, cogs in a much greater machine. The Renaissance was thought to be the era in which the "individual" was born.

Scholars who study the Middle Ages today know that this assessment is completely wrong. Medieval people were writing vivid autobiographies as early as the twelfth century, and we have countless stories of people from all walks of life who asserted their independence from their families and local communities. Many of them may have felt the social pressures of those communities strongly—you can see the same thing in many religious, geographic, or cultural communities today. But that does not mean that people who feel social pressures have no individuality.

This is important, because thinking of medieval people as "cogs in a machine" is a condescending way to view them. Medieval people, like modern people, experienced life through their own subjective encounters. While those experiences were, in important ways, different from our own, medieval people themselves were more like you than you might care to admit.

MYTH: IMPORTANT MEDIEVAL PEOPLE WERE STRAIGHT AND MALE

BEING A woman in the Middle Ages was undoubtedly more difficult than being a man. There were no equal rights for women enshrined into law (although it might be noted that women's rights are not enshrined in American law either, since the requisite 38 states have yet to ratify the Equal Rights Amendment).[12] Medieval women were forbidden from certain occupations, like the priesthood. When women were abused or raped, the law gave them some recourse, but not much. The power behind a woman's word largely depended on her social status. The punishment for raping a woman also varied quite a bit: it might be castration, execution, or a simple fine. But medieval women were far from powerless. They were not the damsels locked in towers that you find in fairy tales. And while many may have found themselves in difficult situations, as with any oppressed population, they found ways to prosper within or resist the system.

Women were active in a number of professions in the Middle Ages. They joined guilds, brewed beer, ran inns, governed land, made and sold textiles, farmed, cooked, and cleaned for a living. There were female blacksmiths, artists, poets, and traveling bards (the men were known as troubadours, the women as trobairitz). Medieval women were not full-time stay-at-home parents, and "housekeeping" often included farming, manual labor, and business endeavors like making candles, soap, or ale. Even the wealthiest women did not live lives of total leisure. Many medieval noblewomen were highly educated. They read and wrote, and some joined the Church as nuns and abbesses, becoming scholars who had a great deal of power and influence. In fact, despite the modern belief that the Church was a fundamental agent of women's oppression in the Middle Ages, more than a few women joined the Church so they could evade marriage and motherhood, preferring instead a life of education, politics, or travel. There was even something of a crisis in twelfth-century France when too many women were choosing to marry the Church rather than a husband.

You might know about a few extraordinary medieval women who led battles, like Joan of Arc, or who led countries, like the Empress Matilda. But you probably missed Olga of Kiev, who led armies to destroy her late husband's enemies and helped bring Christianity to Russia, or Æthelflæd, who fought off the Vikings in Mercia, or Raziya, Sultana of Delhi in the 1200s. Women practiced medicine in the Middle Ages too. Female physician Trota of Salerno wrote important medical treatises on everything from wound treatments to gynecology.[13] As medicine became increasingly professionalized (and elitist) with the establishment of universities, women were gradually pushed out of the profession, but they still practiced their skills as village healers or midwives well into the Renaissance.[14] And the medieval midwife wasn't just responsible for helping women give birth: she had the skills to heal a number of different ailments.

Medieval women were also influential in literature and the arts. Eleanor of Aquitaine and her daughter Marie de Champagne were responsible for sponsoring the Courtly Love movement and helped bring us the Arthurian legends that are still popular today. Marie de France gave us books of *lais* (short chivalric poems), fables, and a story of Saint Patrick. Murasaki Shikibu wrote the world's first novel, *The Tale of Genji*, in eleventh-century Japan. Julian of Norwich and Catherine of Siena were also important writers and theologians.

We could go on and on, but our point is that medieval women doing things that seem "extraordinary" in a patriarchal time is the rule, not the exception. Moreover, medieval women were well aware that they were treated unfairly, and they analyzed and critiqued their own oppression. Christine de Pizan wrote an extensive defense of women called *The Book of the City of Ladies* in response to one of the world's most misogynistic poems, *The Romance of the Rose*. Hrostvitha of Gandersheim, a prolific tenth-century writer, rewrote the ancient comic Terence's plays to make the female characters more heroic and virtuous.

Finally, not all medieval women, and not all medieval men, were straight. Although sexual identity did not exist in quite the same way that it does now, same-sex attraction, love, sex, and relationships were very much a part of the Middle Ages. Records of same-sex relationships can be found across the entire medieval world, from the Middle East to the shores of Iceland and everywhere between. And in some of those places, you can even find examples of same-sex unions formalized by Christian rites. Of course, we don't always know what medieval people were doing behind closed doors. But in some cases, we do—such as in the relationship between King Edward II of England and his lover Piers Gaveston. Al-Hakam II, the second Caliph of Cordoba, married a woman and had two children, but also openly kept a harem of men. And same-sex love wasn't limited to the nobility: in the Middle Ages, priests were issued manuals to help them receive confessions and assign appropriate penances for same-sex acts.

We also have evidence of medieval people who lived as a gender other than the one they were assigned at birth. Some monks and even several saints—such as Saint Marinos—lived their lives as men even though they were born female. Stories have also emerged from court records of men living as women, such as fourteenth-century John Rykener, an English person who sometimes dressed and lived as Eleanor and slept with both men and women. But because we only have the words of the court, we don't know if John preferred being Eleanor or switched between genders as they wanted. We do know that the court doesn't quite know what to make of the situation, and thus, neither do we—except to know that not all medieval people accepted a simple gender binary.

Literature also gives us stories of people living outside normative gender rules—*Yde et Olive* is an old French chivalric story of a girl who becomes a knight, marries a princess, and, by the end, through an angel's intervention, conceives a child with their wife. *Silence* tells the story of a girl who becomes the best male knight in all the realm in order to subvert an unjust law that disinherited women.

History has privileged the stories of straight, cisgender men for so long that it is important to call attention to stories that do not conform to that expectation. Otherwise, people feel as though those with less power in a society don't matter—not just that their stories will be forgotten, but worse, that they deserve to be forgotten.

MYTH: THE MEDIEVAL WORLD WAS WHITE AND CHRISTIAN

MOST MEDIEVAL-THEMED books, games, and shows take place in a generic, castle-and-dragon-strewn, white European setting. But during the historical Middle Ages, a massive hemispherical trade network emerged between Europe, the Middle East, China, Africa, and many points between and beyond. Centers of learning, industry, and culture developed across the Middle East and Asia. The bulk of the world's political, military, economic, and technological power existed outside Europe, which, relatively speaking, was a backwater—a fascinating backwater worth ample study, but a backwater nonetheless.

Medieval Europe itself was far more diverse than most people know. Inevitably, when shows like the BBC's *Merlin* or movies like *Thor* cast non-white actors as characters drawn from European legends, or when shows like *Outlaw King* or *1066: The Battle for Middle Earth* place Black people in medieval Europe, the backlash is as fierce as it is predictable.[15]

Internet trolls converge to complain, claiming either that medieval Europeans were all white or that non-white people were such a small proportion of medieval Europe that they should be ignored in depictions of the period. To people who cling to the myth of an all-white Middle Ages, anything to the contrary is "revisionist" or the work of "social justice warriors." But if anything, excluding people of color from depictions of medieval Europe is the revisionist work, which relies on an outdated perception of medieval Europe as a place that did not change, had no contact with the outside world, and whose people were homogenous.

How many people of color lived in medieval Europe? That is impossible to know for certain. We do have many accounts of people of color in medieval Europe, depictions of people of color in medieval art, and records of regular travel between Europe and the Middle East, Asia, and Africa. For example, Santiago de Compostela in Spain was (and still is) one of the most popular pilgrimage destinations in Europe. And, helpfully for us, we have some records of the names and places of origin of visitors to the site. Many are from Europe, but some are from places like Nubia, Turkey, and from even further afield.

Most of the people who came to European countries from other places were travelers and traders, meaning that any depiction of medieval European urban centers like Rome, Constantinople, Paris, or even far-flung London should include racial diversity. Their appearance would not surprise anyone along popular merchant roads or pilgrimage routes. In order to find places where medieval people of color did not travel or live in Europe, you have to look at small, provincial places. You would have to exclude anywhere the Vikings settled, since their trading empire, at its height, stretched from the Middle East to the Americas. You would also have to exclude Italy and Spain, which had regular interaction with Arabic cultures.

Religious diversity existed in the Middle Ages as well. Medieval Christians were very familiar with people who did not worship the way they did—and not just because of the Crusades. In Al-Andalus (the Arabic term for medieval Iberia), Christians, Jews, and Muslims lived alongside one another. They also lived side by side in the Byzantine Empire and in cities like Damascus and Baghdad. "Saracen" (a medieval term for Muslim) heroes can be found across medieval literature. In fact, several of King Arthur's knights are Saracens—Sir Palomides, Sir Safir, and Sir Segwarides were Muslim. And at least one Arthurian hero, Sir Moriaen, was Black.

We will never know exactly how many people of color visited and lived in medieval Europe. But we do know that even the western Middle Ages were much more diverse than you were led to believe, especially in southern Europe, which was a cosmopolitan center of racial and religious diversity. The fantasy of a white, Christian medieval past is a dangerously antiquated myth that has more to do with what some white people *want* the Middle Ages to have been than what they actually were.

MYTH: THE MIDDLE AGES ARE ANCIENT HISTORY

As WE hope you've realized by now, the Middle Ages still have a lot of relevance today. Maybe too much relevance. In fact, the rest of this book will examine the ways people use myths about Middle Ages to promote retrograde and horrific ideas in the present. Nationalists pretend the medieval past had secure, impenetrable borders, static populations, and firm identities. They use these myths to attack people they label outsiders. Racists idealize an all-white medieval world that never was. Sexists try to lock women up in metaphorical towers by arguing that medieval princesses were the happiest girls of all and that being out of the workforce and stuck at home is a woman's natural place. Religious fanatics think they're following in medieval footsteps when they attack people of other faiths and argue for theocratic government.

None of these myths have very much to do with the Middle Ages. But they have everything to do with the people who interpret the Middle Ages and imbue them with meaning. To some degree, that's part of the power of the Middle Ages: it's a thousand years of the past, containing millions of lives and countless stories. Just as the term *Middle Ages* is, in fact, plural, there was no one, singular, identifiable medieval time. This is true of other time periods as well. But no other time is mythologized in quite such stark terms as the medieval period. No one else in history is seen as so pure, or so filthy. No period has been made so monolithic, so one-dimensional, so "epic." That is why studying the Middle Ages, with all its richness and complexity, can be so rewarding—and why playing with the Middle Ages has so many pitfalls.

2

NATIONALISM AND NOSTALGIA

They say it's a medieval solution, a wall. It's true, because it worked then and it works even better now.
—President Donald J. Trump, 2019[1]

NATIONS THRIVE on stories: stories about why they exist, who founded them, and what their place in the world is. Many people in medieval England believed they were descended from the ancient Trojans, and that a Trojan exile named Brutus discovered Britain with the help of the goddess Diana. In Chaucer's time, some people even considered renaming London *Troynovant*—"New Troy." Tourists in Italy can wander past statues of Romulus and Remus, the mythical founders of Rome, in the city square or see their iconic images—two infants suckled by a she-wolf—tiled into church floors. And of course, there are the stories America tells itself: about a president who could never tell a lie or about Christopher Columbus "discovering" a new world.

So, if all nations have inspirational or even fantastical myths about their origins, meant to inspire patriotism among their citizens, what's the problem? Well, in each of these examples—Washington, Columbus, Brutus, and even Romulus and Remus—a nation's heroes inspire not just patriotism but nationalism. Patriotism can be as simple as pride in one's country. But nationalism isn't a neutral attachment to a preferred place. Nationalism relies on defining *a people*, based on factors that include race, religion, culture, and language. These categories are rarely demarcated by geographical borders, meaning that nationalists turn on people in their own countries in the misguided belief that certain people aren't "loyal" citizens or just don't "belong." Nationalists also argue for their own global superiority, often with violent consequences for their neighbors. In other words, nationalism inevitably leads to war—either within a nation's borders, against other countries, or both.

Rome's nationalist myths motivated its armies to conquer most of Europe and parts of Africa and Asia Minor, dominating and ultimately burying many of the rich cultures that thrived in those places. Brutus became an avatar of the British colonial project, with its legacy of war, violence, cultural suppression, and slavery. The narrative that European explorers "discovered" a new world in the Americas was used to cover up the deaths of millions of Indigenous peoples, and still threatens Indigenous cultures today. And despite the fact that many nationalist movements tout their own modernity and progress, they often root their historical sense of self in the medieval period.

Scholars disagree about whether the kingdoms, empires, and other political states that existed before the modern era can properly be called a "nation." Historian Benedict Anderson, for instance, believes that medieval institutions like the Catholic Church precluded medieval states from being geographically limited and sovereign in the way modern nations are today.[2] Modern states are assumed to be broadly in control of their own affairs, whereas the medieval Church was thought to have acted as a coequal (or even superior) government authority—although, as you'll see in Chapter Six, the Church had far less power than you might think. But regardless of academic quibbling about the definition of a nation, few can argue that when it comes to *imagined* national histories, the Middle Ages play a prominent role. From the English Defence League spreading leaflets festooned with medieval knights and crusaders, to Vladimir Putin erecting statues to his tenth-century namesake Prince Vladimir the Great to boost Russians' patriotic fervor, to French conservative leader Marine Le Pen giving speeches in front of statues of Joan of Arc, medieval symbolism is vital to nationalist sympathies.[3]

A NATIONAL FAIRY TALE

OVER A century before the Holocaust, a strident nationalism swept through Europe, one with which racism, antisemitism, and medievalism became inextricably entangled during a period known as the Romantic Revival.

As a literary and artistic movement, the Romantic Revival was a reaction against neoclassicism. Renaissance Europe had embraced the art, poetry, philosophy, and science of ancient Greece and Rome. But as the Industrial Revolution churned ahead, the Romantics rebelled against the prior generations. They rejected classical forms as artificial and restrained, and they sought to replace them with something they felt was more authentic, that would bring them closer to the "natural" state of humanity, with a greater emphasis on emotion and passion. For many artists, this meant going back to the Middle Ages.

The Romantic Revival brought the world beautiful, poignant poetry and art as well as the liberationist spirit that led to the French Revolution, and, eventually, the abolition of slavery. But Romanticism also had a conservative side, in which pride in national history turned into nationalist propaganda. Many Romantics believed the medieval past was the truest, strongest, and purest spirit of European people. Politically speaking, this meant a rejection of cultural influences that came from the Roman Empire and an embrace of medieval heroes like Siegfried and King Arthur, who were considered proud pre-Roman or even anti-Roman figures.

The ancient Roman Empire was famous not just for geographical conquest but also cultural conquest, via a process that philosopher José Ortega y Gasset called "amalgamation."[4] Rome installed native, local governors to rule over their own people and send tributes back to Rome. Ancient Celtic and Germanic gods were incorporated into the Roman pantheon or merged with their Roman equivalents, and local festivals were transformed into Roman holidays. During the

Middle Ages, the Roman Catholic Church would convert much of Europe to Christianity using the same formula— Michael the Archangel was popular in medieval Iceland, for instance, because of his similarity to Sigurd the dragon-slayer. (In fact, medieval priests had to contend with troublesome locals who kept erecting statues to Michael and paying more attention to him than they did to Christ.) Thanks to a newly awakened nationalism, some Europeans in the eighteenth and nineteenth centuries began to view this Roman influence and alteration of earlier European ways of life as a kind of cultural genocide. For them, the return to the Middle Ages was a recovery project.

One place you might be surprised to find this cocktail of nationalism and Romantic nostalgia is in the Grimm Brothers' fairy tales. The Brothers Grimm were two German siblings who worked to compile German and Norse folk stories. Jacob Grimm, in particular, was committed to recovering these tales not just as a literary or aesthetic venture but as a form of cultural and national mythography—a way of tracing all the legends and stories from the past that had been lost. He conceived of his research and writing as primarily nationalistic, an effort to help Germans free themselves from the influence of Rome and form their own identity: in his 1848 *History of the German Language*, Grimm lauded ancient Germans for bringing down the Roman empire and granting "fresh freedom to the Romans in Gaul, Italy, Spain, and Britain," and medieval Germans for ensuring Christianity's dominance in Europe "by erecting an unbreakable wall against the constantly pressing Slavs in Europe's middle."[5]

A key part of nationalist ideologies, both in the Romantic period and today, is the belief that each nation has a particular, well-defined "spirit." The Grimms saw the tales they collected as representative of the German soul. Wilhelm Grimm compiled Danish stories, claiming that they—and other Scandinavian myths—were "Germanic" at their core. He is quoted in the introduction to the 1944 edition of the Grimm

Brothers' *Fairy Tales* as saying, "I strove to penetrate into the wild forests of our ancestors ... listening to their whole language, and watching their pure customs."[6]

And the Grimm Brothers didn't just compile fairy tales. Jacob Grimm undertook literary expeditions to recover medieval German grammar, Germanic mythology, and "proto-Germanic" languages in order to restore the "essence" of what it meant to be German. He proposed that many northern European languages had Germanic roots, and he probed Norse mythology for its possible Germanic connections. Thus, the Grimms didn't just tell stories; they were key figures in a reinterpretation of language, myth, and literature that sought to place the German people at the core of European culture.

The Grimm Brothers' works, and their assertions of a medieval Germanic identity (called pan-Germanic by scholars), were also rooted in a nation-building project. During their lifetime, Germany was not the unified country that we know today but a loose collection of competing kingdoms, principalities, and duchies. Their assertion of a pan-Germanic identity with deep historical roots had the explicitly political aim of arguing that these smaller states should be one unified nation. The German nation-building project came to fruition with the unification of Germany in 1871 but that was hardly the end of German nationalism.

For instance, Richard Wagner's 1876 opera cycle *Der Ring des Nibelungen* (*The Ring of the Nibelung*), based on the Icelandic *Völsunga Saga* and the German *Niebelungenlied*, became an unofficial German national epic and a core part of German identity. Its hero was Siegfried, known as "Sigurd" in Old Norse or "Sîvrit" in Middle High German. Siegfried was depicted as a model of medieval masculinity and "Germanic" spirit. Here he is introduced in *Völsunga Saga*, Chapter 23, as Sigurd:

> Sigurd's hair was brown and splendid to see. It fell in
> long locks. His beard, of the same color, was thick and

short. His eyes flashed so piercingly that few dared to look
beneath his brow. His shoulders were as broad as if one
were looking at two men.... It is a mark of his great height
that when he girded himself with his sword Gram, which
was seven spans long, and waded through a field of full-
grown rye, the tip of the sword's sheath grazed the top of
the standing grain. And his strength exceeded his stature.[7]

Siegfried is known for various feats of courage and strength,
including, in some stories, slaying the dragon Fafnir. He vari-
ously drinks dragon's blood, bathes in it, or eats a dragon's
heart to gain supernatural powers like horned skin and the
ability to understand what birds are saying.

Siegfried's physical dominance and outsized masculinity
were also part of his appeal to modern nationalists, since
sexism and nationalism tend to go hand-in-hand. Siegfried's
romantic counterpart is the maiden Brunhild (also called
Prunhilt or Brynhild), a famous warrior woman. In *Völsunga
Saga*, Brunhild has been cursed by Odin, trapped sleeping in
her armor as a punishment for fighting Odin's favorite warrior. In the *Niebelungenlied*, Brunhild is an Icelandic queen
who forces suitors to compete against her in feats of strength,
including boulder-hurling. But Siegfried and Brunhild are not
meant to be. In the *Niebelungenlied*, another man marries
Brunhild against her will but has no success getting his new
wife into bed—at one point, she hangs him from a nail on
the wall when he tries it—so Siegfried disguises himself as
the husband and rapes her. Misogyny undergirds nationalism
to such an extent that his deception and assault of Brunhild,
while horrifying to us and tragic to some medieval writers,
was far from a deal-breaker for nationalists enamored with
his "masculine" prowess.

The medieval Siegfried is a highly flawed hero. He is
eventually murdered, betrayed by his own wife and a close
friend. Readers are led to believe that this is just punishment for his deception of Brunhild. But Wagner cleans up
Siegfried's flaws, revising the story to leave his hero blameless
for Brunhild's rape because he was bewitched by a potion.

Wagner's Brunhild forgives Siegfried, and she and even the gods themselves die with him at the end of the opera as Valhalla is destroyed.

Wagner's nineteenth-century version of Siegfried—a Nordic-Germanic, übermasculine warrior beloved by the gods—became the avatar of German nationalism that would be adopted by the Third Reich's massive neomedieval propaganda campaign. There was even a "Camp Siegfried" on Long Island, New York, in the 1930s that turned out to be a Nazi training facility in disguise! But Siegfried's failures were important to German nationalism too. His fatal flaws—lust, drunkenness, and disloyalty—served as a warning: allow yourself to be corrupted by femininity and weakness, or turn your back on your people, and you could be responsible for the downfall of the German people.

ONCE AND FUTURE KINGS

GERMANS WEREN'T the only ones to embrace nationalist medievalism in the 1800s. Britain used the Middle Ages to prop up its own nationalist and colonial projects as well. Prior to the nineteenth century, "British" identity was somewhat fragmented. Wales was annexed by England in the 1500s; Scotland and England unified in 1707; Ireland was incorporated into the United Kingdom in 1801. The United Kingdom is still comprised of these four distinct nations (though most Irish won their independence, and only Northern Ireland remains) and remains a tapestry of local and regional identities. But over the course of the nineteenth century, nationalists in the UK attempted to forge a single identity out these many component parts—particularly in England and Scotland. And like the Germans, they turned to medieval myths, legends, and heroes to support this ethnic nationalism.

Who better than King Arthur, the legendary hero famous for uniting the warring territories of medieval England under a single crown, to represent this mythical English identity?[8]

Arthur has a very long history of being used to inspire English patriotism. The myth of the Trojan hero Brutus we described earlier eventually entangled itself with the myth of King Arthur during the Middle Ages. In the twelfth century, chroniclers proposed that Arthur was Brutus's descendent, thus connecting the two most famous figures in medieval British lore to each other. As Arthur's ancestry improved, and his importance to England grew, his reported exploits became more impressive. Arthur's legend began with merely a single mention in a ninth-century chronicle as a general who fought the Saxons at the Battle of Badon Hill. But over the centuries, his story accumulated a tragic love affair, a legendary circle of knights, and the Holy Grail. In some medieval legends, Arthur also rebels against Rome by refusing to pay his taxes. (England was required to send "tribute" back to Rome in what would have been Arthur's time.) Emboldened by his own rebellion, Arthur then goes on a conquering spree, taking over England, Iceland, and even Rome itself.

In spite of Arthur's dubious historicity, by the fourteenth century, most prospective English kings had biographies commissioned to "prove" they were descended from both Arthur and Brutus. During the Wars of the Roses—an English civil war in the fifteenth century—Henry Tudor finally united the divided country by convincing the Welsh to back his claim to the throne. Wales was already suppressed under English rule. So how did an English king rally a colonized people to fight his battles for him? One of the tactics he used was to fight under the banner of the Red Dragon, a symbol of King Arthur that is still on the Welsh flag today. Henry Tudor's infamous son Henry VIII argued for his right to divorce (and divorce, and divorce) by claiming that he owed no allegiance to the Roman Catholic Church because his ancestor, King Arthur, had once conquered the Roman Empire. Henry VIII even had his own face painted on Arthur's body on the Winchester Round Table, a supposed relic of King Arthur's court.

All this history and myth made Arthur the perfect avatar for nineteenth-century British nationalism. Alfred Lord

Tennyson, poet laureate for Queen Victoria, drew on this aspect of King Arthur in his 1869 poem "The Coming of Arthur," collected in his *Idylls of the King*:

> For many a petty king ere Arthur came
> Ruled in this isle, and ever waging war
> Each upon other, wasted all the land; [...]
> And after these King Arthur for a space,
> And through the puissance of his Table Round,
> Drew all their petty princedoms under him,
> Their king and head, and made a realm, and reigned.[9]

King Arthur's success in trampling the "petty princedoms" of medieval England into submission fed England's own vision of itself as a colonial power. In many English minds, Arthurian "history" justified their grip on territories like Ireland, Wales, and Scotland, and on colonized peoples further afield, like India, Africa, the Americas, and Australia.

Colonial medievalism was often a hypocritical doctrine: England touted its medieval heroes when it suited them, but they also oppressed the people they conquered by calling *them* "medieval." As historian Thomas R. Metcalf argues, in the nineteenth century the British people viewed India as living in a "medieval" state and argued that its brutal colonial occupation of the subcontinent was an effort to "civilize."[10] It is ironic that Rome, which had once conquered much of Europe, became a focus of hatred and disdain in British and European nations—all while they were busily attacking the culture and traditions of other people around the globe, behaving like a much worse incarnation of the ancient empire they so vehemently rejected.

SCOTLAND THE BRAVE(HEART)

NEOMEDIEVAL NATIONALISM isn't just a feature of the former empires of the world. Sometimes, colonized territories use the Middle Ages to argue for self-rule. For instance, in 1995, the growing cause for Scottish independence from England acquired an unexpected ally: Mel Gibson.[11] The movie *Braveheart* was a huge success. It also resulted in a significant uptick in tourism for Scotland and a surge of Scottish nationalism. In fact, the Scottish National Party (SNP) jumped in the polls almost overnight.

Among medieval historians, *Braveheart* is something of a joke. But it's not just the kilts, the blue face-paint, or the Battle of Stirling Bridge—fought, as it is in the film, with neither the city of Stirling nor a bridge in sight. It's also the way that *Braveheart* mythologizes the Scottish Highlanders as "noble savages," pure and uncorrupted, allegedly representing the essence of their nation.

Braveheart goes to great lengths to promote a single idea of the Highland Scots as the heart of a noble civilization. In the film, the Scottish are a people on the edge of the world, wild, unkempt, barely civilized. But that is fused with a sense that despite their rough edges, they possess ancient wisdom and superior morals. Take the central character, William Wallace: the historical Wallace was a member of the local gentry, but *Braveheart* reimagines him as a rough-and-tumble peasant-warrior. His secret marriage in the film, in the woods before a stone cross rather than in a church, evokes a druidic-mystical tradition that is historically dubious at best but incredibly popular with the neo-pagan "Celtic" revival of the 1980s and 1990s. Wallace's mystical connection to the land is reinforced in the many scenes with lengthy shots of vast, craggy scenery backed by mournful bagpipes, or the montage of Wallace climbing through the mountains. Nationalism often seeks to link people spiritually to the land in which they live—although in *Braveheart*'s case, those shots were filmed in Ireland.

Braveheart's nationalist propaganda depends on the myth that a distinctly Scottish spirit developed in raw, uncorrupted isolation from the rest of the world. But in real life, medieval Scottish and English aristocrats held lands on both sides of the border simultaneously, the lowland Scots and the English across the border were more-or-less indistinguishable, and the highlanders were not that distinct from their cousins across the sea in Ireland.

In the film, Scottish warriors are ruthless on the battle-field, and each of the protagonists ends each battle soaked in English blood. But despite their battlefield ferocity, the Scots are shown to be far more noble than their English counter-parts. Wallace's compatriots are rowdy but good-natured, gen-erous, and kind. By contrast, the English are universally cruel: Gibson himself described the character of the English King Edward I in his film as a "psychopath." (*Outlander* fans will recognize a similar dynamic in the way the television show portrays the English and the Scots.)

In the wake of *Braveheart*'s release, the SNP capitalized on reenergized patriotism with a campaign they called "head and heart" that made use of the film's imagery in its campaign lit-erature. The SNP's leader Andy Salmon called upon the film's climax in the conclusion to his speech at the party's annual conference in 1995: "So that we can say with Wallace—head and heart—the one word which encapsulates all our hopes— *Freedom, Freedom, Freedom.*"[12]

Scotland would not have a referendum on full indepen-dence until 2014. But by that time, the nature of Scottish nationalism had changed: many on the "Yes Scotland" campaign actively distanced themselves from the romantic nostalgia of *Braveheart*, instead hoping to argue the case for independence based on its merits rather than against a bag-pipe-festooned soundtrack. But the referendum failed, and the Scottish people elected to remain part of the United Kingdom, only to be faced two years later with another impassioned separatist movement: Brexit.

WALLS, MOATS, AND DRAGONS

NATIONALISM IS experiencing a reawakening all over the globe, particularly in Europe and the United States. And medi-evalism is part of the movement once again. For instance, the current United Kingdom is an international project: until recently a member of the European Union, it also spans multiple nations, including Scotland, Wales, Northern Ireland, and England. But thanks to virulent, escalating nationalist and populist sentiment, in 2016, the British people narrowly voted to leave the EU. And on 31 January 2020, the United Kingdom officially left the EU.

Many in the Leave Campaign cited medieval grudges to support their newfound British isolationism. Brexit proponent Nigel Farage, for instance, compared Britain's membership in the EU to England's defeat in the Norman Conquest. But one of the strangest features of Brexit was neomedieval propaganda that revolved around Saint George, who, despite being depicted as a heroic medieval knight, was not actually medieval—or British.

Saint George was a half-Greek and half-Palestinian officer in the fourth-century Roman Empire who was executed for his Christian faith. Although George was not medieval, he was wildly popular in the medieval imagination, so much so that medieval people invented an entire chivalric tradition around him, turning him into a knight who rescues a princess and slays a dragon. George became one of the most popular warrior saints in the medieval Christian world. He was venerated by crusaders, and King Edward III named him the patron saint of his Order of the Garter, Edward's much-criticized vehicle for reviving "chivalry."

In twenty-first century England, far-right political parties and hate groups embraced Saint George's symbolic use in the Crusades and used the saint—and his iconic red cross on a white background—as a symbol not just of English patriotism but also of anti-Muslim, anti-immigrant white nationalism. The far-right United Kingdom Independence Party (UKIP) made marking Saint George's Day as a national holiday part of their party platform.[13] The English Defence League (EDL), an Islamophobic organization founded in 2009, uses the cross of Saint George on a shield as their emblem, flanked by the Latin phrase "*in hoc signo vinces*"—meaning "in this sign you shall conquer." At their rallies, EDL members frequently wear face masks adorned with Saint

George's cross, fly banners with their logos superimposed on the flag of England, and wear pins depicting Saint George himself as a crusader with "EDL" on his shield. In 2015, a UKIP candidate for parliament even retweeted an inflammatory cartoon of Saint George lancing the Prophet Mohammed with the caption "Happy St George's Day Infidels."[14]

In the months before the Brexit vote, the campaign to leave the European Union was careful not to directly associate itself with hate groups like the EDL. But there's no doubt that the anti-immigrant rhetoric employed by the Leave campaign was buoyed by the specter of Saint George the "crusader," and may have contributed to Britain's decision to leave the EU and get back to its supposedly medieval nature.

Americans, on the other hand, have long imagined their nation as the antithesis of a certain vision of what "medieval" means: aristocracy, tyranny, and religious oppression. But medievalism has been present in the American cultural and political landscape for generations, and despite America's foundation well after the medieval period, nationalist leaders often rely on misunderstood medieval concepts to promote their agendas.

Recently, the US has seen an almost unprecedented wave of medievalism in political propaganda. This may be a result of the rise of international far-right groups (like the so-called alt-right) that frequently deploy medievalism in their rhetoric and recruiting materials. But it may also be because the same Russian operatives who used online spaces to encourage Brexit relied on similar memes and rhetoric to manipulate nationalist and Islamophobic sentiment in the US and used that propaganda to assist the election of President Donald J. Trump.[15]

Trump has a long legacy of associations with medievalism.[16] Trump even proposed a Madison Avenue apartment building, "Trump Castle," that would have had a drawbridge and a medieval-style moat. (Thankfully, it was never built.) Trump's medievalism is also an integral part of his nationalism, a label he has embraced despite its associations with murderous regimes and the racist and xenophobic groups that emulate them. "I'm a nationalist," Trump declared at a rally in Texas in 2018, while admitting, "we're not supposed to use that word."[17] And he repeatedly invokes the Middle Ages as an expression of his white nationalism. In a 2016 campaign speech, Trump used myths about the Middle Ages to make a case for increased American aggression and even the torture of prisoners. He accused Muslims of being "medieval" and argued that the United States should get medieval in turn:

> We're living in medieval times. We have to stop it. We have to be so strong. We have to fight so viciously and violently because we're dealing with violent people.... Look, we have laws, and the laws say, you can't do this, you can't do that, you can't do, you know, a lot. Their laws say you can do anything you want and the more vicious you are, the better.... So we can't do waterboarding but they can do chopping off heads, drowning people in steel cages.... we have no leadership. You know, you have to fight fire with fire.[18]

Trump toned down the neomedieval rhetoric during his first two years in power, but in the wake of the 2018 midterm elections, in which his party lost control of the House of Representatives, Trump returned to his campaign medievalism. He had been pushing the idea of building a wall on the US border with Mexico since the first days of his 2016 campaign, even promising that Mexico would pay for it.

But after the midterm losses, Trump demanded that the wall be built as an emergency priority. Rather than getting Mexico to fund it, Trump demanded money from American taxpayers, forcing the government to shut down for 35 days when he couldn't get his way. Democratic leaders fired back by declaring that the wall was "medieval." Representative Hakeem Jeffries, Senator Dick Durbin, a number of Democratic presidential candidates, and Senator Chuck Schumer (who had been calling the wall "medieval" since 2017) joined the chorus: they all agreed, the wall was "medieval"—meaning it was bad, barbaric, and ineffective.[19] Surprising his critics, Trump embraced that medieval identity: "They say a wall is medieval—well, so is a wheel," he argued. "A wheel is older than a wall. There are some things that work, you know what? A wheel works, and a wall works."[20]

Leaving aside the fact that wheels are not older than walls, this is one of a few examples in contemporary American history of a political figure lauding an idea not in spite of its medieval connotations but because of them. Trump's critics were quick to point out that the wall would be comically ineffective—simple to climb over, to cut through, or to tunnel under. But the wall's medievalism has more to do with its symbolism than its practicality. It reveals the way Trump and his most fervent supporters want to see the United States: as a neomedieval fortress, protected from the people who might alter the American national "spirit." For Trump's most fervent supporters, the idea of a "medieval wall" evoked a distinctly different image from the one that Democratic critics saw. Those who celebrated the wall wanted America not to be what Ronald Reagan famously called "a shining city on a hill"—a beacon that is as inviting as it is inspiring.[21] Instead they wanted it to be a fortified castle protected by dragons and a moat.

In order for the country to require the wall, dragons, and moat, there has to be a "medieval" threat. In the days prior to the 2018 midterm election, Trump and many Republican candidates used rhetoric that recast groups of poor refugees fleeing violence on foot from Honduras, Guatemala, and El Salvador into caravans of "invaders" and "terrorists." Unfounded rumors on hate sites like *Breitbart* and *Infowars*, and repeated by the president himself, warned that these caravans included Muslim terrorists and members of the notorious gang MS-13.[22] This mix of misinformation was meant to make Americans feel as though they were under siege by an invading medieval horde. Trump supporters could thus envision themselves as righteous heroes defending their homes.

Now, the rhetoric most of the media found amusing and silly has horrifying and deadly consequences: less than one year after Trump's call for a "medieval wall," the United States began locking up adults and children who came seeking asylum in overcrowded cells, deprived of basic human needs like water, food, and beds, and even simple items like toothpaste. Inflamed by Trump's propaganda and their own racism, immigration agents are even seizing American citizens who "look" like immigrants.[23] Both adults and children have died from these conditions, and many more will suffer unless the administration is stopped.[24]

NATIONALIST MEDIEVALISMS AROUND THE WORLD

Despite the popularity of medievalism in Europe and the United States, the penchant for medievalist nationalism is hardly limited to these areas. Vladimir Putin's fervently nationalist regime in Russia has also turned to the Middle Ages for inspiration. In 2016, Putin erected a statue of Prince Vladimir the Great, tenth-century founder of Eastern Orthodox Christianity, in Moscow. Calling the elder Vladimir the "spiritual founder of the Russian State," Putin used the statue's unveiling to honor Russia's power and expansionism.[25] As we have shown so far, it isn't easy to separate nationalism from racism, misogyny, and xenophobia, and Putin's nationalism is no different. Alongside his "patriotic" medieval revival, Putin has called multiculturalism "untenable," rolled back women's rights, and incited hatred against European immigrants, saying that they "kill, plunder, and rape with impunity."[26] The idea that Russia has racially or religiously homogenous roots in the Middle Ages is completely wrong: medieval Russia was made up of Scandinavians, Slavs, Mongols, Turks, Jews, Tatars, and many other groups. It was far from insular in ethnicity, language, or faith. And many important medieval Russian figures were women. But the truth rarely matters in nationalist narratives.

In increasingly authoritarian Turkey, the medieval television drama *Ertugrul*, taglined "A Nation's Awakening," is incredibly popular. *Ertugrul* tells the story of the founder of the Ottoman Empire in sweeping, heroic glory. The show's popularity coincides with the rise of far-right nationalist President Erdoğan, who has used medieval nostalgia to promote nationalism and revive several Ottoman traditions. He even has his guards dress in Ottoman costume.[27] In Brazil, as Paulo Pachá wrote in a February 2019 exposé for *Pacific Standard*, the new far-right, nationalist administration under president Jair Bolsonaro has been using *Deus Vult*—"God wills it," a rallying cry attributed to the Crusades—as its slogan. Popular videos produced by Bolsonaro's supporters have titles like, "Brazil: The Last Crusade" and "The Cross and the Sword," using the Crusades to promote Brazil's "European" national heritage.[28]

Leaders who fetishize the Middle Ages tend not only to have nationalist agendas but also authoritarian ones. Politicians manipulate medieval nostalgia to demand loyalty to the state, to break international agreements and alliances, and, ultimately, to suppress their own people. They claim to do this in favor of replacing "globalism" with "patriotism," and try to justify hatred, harassment, and violence by touting a national medieval past. Nationalist medievalism believes that it is returning its people to a past that is "safer" by shutting out anything it deems foreign to what it decides is its original essence. Not only is this propaganda racist and often deadly, it's also not medieval. Because medieval people were anything but insular.

THE COSMOPOLITAN MIDDLE AGES

THE MEDIEVAL world was far more interconnected and cosmopolitan than many people realize. Some scholars argue that the medieval period heralded the beginning of globalism—or at the very least, a hemispherism that saw greater and greater interactions between Europe, Asia, and Africa.[29] Western Europe was part of this burgeoning hemispherical world, but it was not at the center of it. In fact, if you look at maps of the world from the eighth century to the fifteenth, you'll be struck by just how tiny western Europe seems compared to the empires, caliphates, and kingdoms in the rest of the world. Far more powerful and influential were the Chinese dynasties; the Byzantine Empire that ringed the Mediterranean and Black Seas; the Muslim caliphates across the Middle East, Africa, and Europe; and the Mongol empire that stretched from the Pacific Ocean to the Mediterranean. As professor of anthropology at American University Chapurukha Kusimba put it in a 2017 interview with *The Public Medievalist,*

> I think many historians and economic historians now characterize the period from the Tang dynasty in the 8th century to the end of the Ming Dynasty in the 16th as the period when Asia was the world. In many ways Asian empires, including the Islamic Caliphates, China, and India, were economically and politically powerful. At the time, the world revolved around them.... Commerce between the Mediterranean world and Southern Europe, North Africa, East Africa, South Asia, and East Asia was regular—the entire region was completely intertwined.[30]

This network—one in which the Middle East, India, China, and Mongolia formed a center of trade, culture, research, and political power—puts Europe on the periphery.

For centuries, American and European writers and filmmakers have reversed this formula, portraying non-Western medieval cultures as practically barbaric. (The 1999 film

Thirteenth Warrior, based loosely on a Muslim writer's encounter with Vikings in the tenth century, is a notable exception.) Medieval Mongols on film and television are portrayed as a horde of fearsome barbarians—the Dothraki in *Game of Thrones* are clearly an analogue. But while the Mongols conquered a vast portion of the world, their depiction as uncivilized rapists and murderers has more to do with the fear and propaganda spread by their European opponents than by actual history. The real Mongol Empire promoted religious tolerance and safety for civilians across their territories, meaning people could travel from Europe to China in relative peace. Trade and education flourished across the Mongol Empire due to this ability to move freely. Marco Polo famously documented his travels along the Silk Road, but it was the Mongol Empire that made the Silk Road possible.[31]

And yet, although medieval Europe was less important than other areas of the globe, it was not isolated. We have ample records of people from the Middle East and sub-Saharan Africa coming to Europe to trade, learn, and settle. Southern Europe—especially Spain, Sicily, and the Byzantine Empire—hosted travelers, traders, and migrants from across the Mediterranean.[32] We have records of sub-Saharan African travelers too: in the beginning of the fifteenth century, Ethiopian embassies sprang up all around southern Europe and grew into burgeoning communities.[33]

Moreover, Europe itself was cosmopolitan, with people traveling back and forth between cultures—and not just for war. Al-Andalus (medieval Iberia, now Spain) was right next to France, and North Africa was right across the Mediterranean. Both were relatively easy to travel to. Parts of France were sometimes ruled by England, and vice versa. Western European culture relied heavily on the philosophical, literary, commercial, and scientific exchanges they had with people in the Middle East. To this list of cosmopolitan and multicultural societies, one can add Norman Sicily, the Byzantine Empire, medieval Indonesia, and even Viking Scandinavia.

Vikings, despite being imagined as a "pure" culture by racists, were some of the most well-traveled, curious, and non-insular people in northern Europe. Needless to say, Viking depictions in contemporary popular culture bear only passing resemblance to actual history. First of all, there's no such thing as a "Viking," at least not in the Middle Ages. Scholars aren't sure exactly how the term emerged, but most agree that the word is revivalist, coined by the same nineteenth-century medieval-infatuated writers we discussed earlier in the chapter.[34] It may be tied to Old Norse or Old English root words for "sea" or "camp." Historically, the people we have come to call "Vikings" constituted a wide variety of groups, each with its own cultural identity, religious practices, and way of life.[35]

As a result, there is no such thing as "Viking culture." What we see on television and in video games as "Viking" culture is a pastiche of medieval Scandinavian, Anglo-Saxon, and Germanic cultures. They traded with, raided, and conquered places as far-flung as Iceland, France, Sicily, Greece, and Russia. They didn't wear those horned helmets either—those came into style about 800 years too late for a "Viking" to wear. Drawn by Scandinavian artists in the 1800s, the horned helmet became canonical Viking gear when Wagner used it in the same Siegfried operas we discussed above.

A medieval "Viking's" entire way of life was based upon international, intercultural, and interreligious interaction. Some of those interactions were violent, to be sure, but most were not. If Vikings can be said to have built an empire, it was an empire of trade and commerce. And instead of seeing their ways as inherently superior, Vikings were famously willing to adopt and adapt to the local customs of the places they went. Vikings conquered and colonized Normandy in the tenth century. But within a few generations, they were completely indistinguishable from the local populace. The same happened in Sicily—in the eleventh century, the newly Norman Vikings conquered Sicily, and quickly integrated with the local population. For the remainder of the book, we'll use the term *Viking* out of convenience, but keep in mind that when we use it, we're referring to a group of people based on their activities and interactions with other cultures, not on a shared cultural identity.

THE MYTH OF "PURE" MEDIEVAL NATIONS

BEGINNING IN the eighteenth century, thanks to pseudo-scientific and pseudohistorical race theories, many white English and American people began to identify as racially "Anglo-Saxon." In fact, in 2014, American presidential candidate Mitt Romney touted a shared "Anglo-Saxon heritage" as the reason his White House would a have better relationship with Britain than Barack Obama's.[36] This is a peculiar bit of historical sleight of hand, given the incredibly diverse and mixed heritage not just of modern America but also of medieval Britain.

When the Roman Empire first set out to conquer "Britannia," it was populated by a range of tribes—including Celts, Picts, Gauls, and Belgae. Archaeological evidence suggests that these tribes were already trading with the Irish, Gallic, and Germanic tribes on the European continent. They even sold tin in Mediterranean ports.[37] After a series of attempted and failed conquests, the Romans took over much of Britain from the first to the fifth century. Keep in mind that at this point, Romans themselves had already assimilated Greek, African, Middle Eastern, and other cultural practices, beliefs, and peoples. While Romans ruled in Britain, they faced periodic invasions by what chroniclers call "barbarians": Frankish, Saxon, and Gallic raiders, as well as the Picts, Scots, and Irish, and the Attacotti, whose origins are unknown. Romans also hired mercenaries to fight off these invasions, bringing in Vandal and Germanic warriors to aid their cause.

Rome pulled out of Britain by the fifth century, and Britain would then be fought over again: between the Romanized Britons; the native forces of what would become Ireland, Scotland, and Wales; and the invading Saxons, Angles, Jutes, and other Germanic peoples. The Saxons won out in the short run, and by the eighth century, they ruled much of England.

This is the point at which modern nationalists—especially the ones who want to call themselves "Anglo-Saxons"—would have you believe that England now had a stable, singular cultural identity. This is when they spoke "Old English," after all, a catch-all term used to describe multiple dialects. But even aside from all the different cultures and peoples that had already coalesced in England over the centuries, the Saxons also had to reckon with Vikings, who continually showed up to raid, settle, and sometimes knock Saxon kings off their thrones. Vikings didn't just bring their warriors to England, they brought all the cultural influences and artifacts they had from their seafaring exploration and trade. If England ever really had been "pure"—which, as you can see, it hadn't—Vikings would have quickly put an end to that.

Finally, in 1066, after a long showdown between the Saxon and Danish royalty, the Norman French (who had also been conquered by Vikings) arrived to complicate English identity even more. William the Bastard of Normandy won the battle for the English throne and gained a much nicer nickname, William the Conqueror. At this point, England became French—or at least, French-ish. The island was ruled by Normans, who integrated with the local populace and created a hybrid language—Anglo-Norman—from which modern English eventually arose. By the twelfth century, England was a mix of Norman French culture—which was already a mixture of Roman, German, Norse, Breton, and other cultures—and Anglo-Saxon culture, which was a mix of German, Norse, Roman, Celtic and other cultures. Oh, and the Roman Catholic Church was constantly bringing people from abroad to the shores of the island. Chaucer's Middle English, a language that arose from the blending of Old English and Old French languages, was just one of the many simultaneous dialects of the English language that slowly grew out of the Norman Conquest. And there were at least 400 more years of war, invasion, trade, conquest, exploration, conversion, and other interactions that would keep changing the shape and the nature of what we know of as "England" when the Middle Ages drew to a close.

The mixture of cultures we just traced in medieval England is not a historical exception. It's the rule. The nation we now call Germany was inhabited by different Germanic tribes, but also by Romans, French, the Huns, and many others. Parts of medieval Iberia were ruled by a Muslim caliphate in the early Middle Ages, a center of power and trade that brought people and cultures from across the Islamic world and the Byzantine Empire. When Iberia was slowly conquered by Christian kingdoms in the latter half of the Middle Ages, it retained much of this diversity. And throughout the medieval period, French, Spanish, English, and German nobility all regularly intermarried. We even have evidence of marriages between medieval Christians and Muslims.

Nationalists from the nineteenth century onward imagine that the medieval world not only had concrete, rigid geographical borders but firm ethnic borders as well. As you can see, this is complete nonsense. That's not to say that there were no differences or conflicts between medieval kingdoms and countries—there were plenty. But medieval people lacked the sense of international enmity that seems to drive so many of our deepest conflicts today, both inside nations and between them.

3

THE "CLASH OF CIVILIZATIONS"

> In its moments of great achievement, medieval culture positively thrived on holding at least two, and often many more, contrary ideas at the same time.
>
> —María Rosa Menocal, *The Ornament of the World*, 2002[1]

ON 27 July 2011, Anders Behring Breivik murdered 77 people in Norway, driven by his ethnonationalist hatred of Muslim immigrants. On 29 January 2017, Alexandre Bissonnette murdered six Muslim men in a Quebec City mosque because he feared that "non-white, non-European immigration" would "lead to the marginalization of whites."[2] On 27 October 2018, Robert Bowers murdered 11 Jewish worshippers at the Tree of Life synagogue in Pittsburgh, Pennsylvania, saying he wanted "all Jews to die."[3] He believed—thanks to President Trump's own rhetoric[4]—that Jews were funding a caravan of refugees from South America to cause a white genocide. And on 15 March 2019, white supremacist terrorist Brenton Tarrant killed 51 people and injured 49 more at a mosque and an Islamic Center in Christchurch, New Zealand, simultaneously releasing a manifesto called "The Great Replacement," which warned of genocide against white people.

What do any of these incidents have to do with medievalism or the misuse of medieval history? A great deal, as it turns out. Breivik considered himself a modern-day crusader and wrote a 1508-page manifesto that he titled *2083: A European Declaration of Independence.* He railed against Islam, multiculturalism, and feminism, and claimed to be a leader of the New Order of the Knights Templar, Europe.[5]

Bissonnette posted crusader knight images on his Facebook page alongside his racist screeds. The paranoia behind Robert Bowers' killing spree came directly from Nazi propaganda; the Nazis used medieval antisemitic stereotypes to paint Jewish people as outsiders who could "contaminate" a nation by increasing immigration. And the Christchurch shooter scrawled names and dates all over his weapons in white paint: among other right-wing hate symbols and the names of modern-day killers who had murdered Muslims and migrants, he also painted multiple references to the Middle Ages. This included the name of medieval military leader Charles Martel, along with other figures who have also been lionized by the extreme-right for their participation in the Crusades or their wars against the Ottoman Empire. His manifesto claims that he contacted the "reborn Knights Templar for a blessing in support of the attack, which was given," and it repeatedly invokes the Crusades in all capitals: "ASK YOURSELF: WHAT WOULD POPE URBAN II DO?" and "UNTIL THE HAGIA SOPHIA IS FREE OF THE MINARETS, THE MEN OF EUROPE ARE MEN IN NAME ONLY."[6]

Medievalism has a long and deadly history of being used in antisemitic and Islamophobic propaganda. White supremacists view the Middle Ages as a heroic and glorious time not in spite of horrors like the Crusades and the widespread violence against Jews, but because of them. They believe they are continuing a medieval struggle—whether that's the so-called Aryan medieval hero's struggle against the gods or the Christian crusaders' holy wars. And their obsessions have inspired not only the violent killers we listed above but massive state-sponsored genocide, including in Nazi Germany.

As you will see throughout the book, racism, sexism, homophobia, ableism, and religious discrimination are often a feature of white supremacist violence. With antisemitism and Islamophobia in particular, the line between racism and religious discrimination can be very blurry. Anti-Muslim violence has been directed against Sikhs, Hindus, and anyone else who "looks" Muslim.[7] Both Muslims and Jews are regularly accused of global conspiracies that threaten to take the world "backwards."[8] Both have been accused of being "medieval," and both have been persecuted by people trying to live out warped medieval fantasies. All this hatred and paranoia often has little to do with actual Jewish or Muslim religious practices. Instead, white supremacists perceive these as *ethnic* identities that are inherently opposed to their own.

MEDIEVALISM IN NAZI GERMANY

THE SAME nationalist medievalisms that swept Europe during the nineteenth century inspired some of the worst war crimes and human rights abuses of the twentieth century. Nationalism's inherent interest in separating people, and in arguing for the superiority of one culture over others, makes it a natural companion to racism, antisemitism, and Islamophobia. In twentieth-century Europe, the nineteenth-century medievalisms that inspired national unity were increasingly conflated with the illusion of a pure, white medieval past. These ideological misuses of the Middle Ages aggravated one another in places like Nazi Germany, with deadly consequences.

Medievalism that may have seemed charmingly patriotic when deployed by the Grimm Brothers became an unimaginable horror when pushed to its conclusion: the extermination or domination of all races except the "Germanic ideal" imagined by the Nazi regime.[9] Wagner brought new life to the medieval German *Parsifal* and *Niebelungenlied* at the end of the nineteenth century. But in the twentieth century, his operas became Nazi propaganda. In the nineteenth century, Wagner had celebrated the heroic Siegfried; a few decades later, the Nazi party adopted him as a model of cultural purity, a hero who could conquer the foe they thought was their primary adversary: a mythical Jewish conspiracy.

Nazis considered all non-white peoples biologically and morally inferior, but they thought Jews were a particularly

sinister racial type that was dangerous to "white purity."
The view of Jewish people as a race requires some clarifica-
tion. Some people, Jewish and otherwise, see Judaism as only
a religion. Others see Judaism as an ethnicity or a culture.
Judaism even has cultural and historical divisions that are
sometimes racialized: between Sephardic and Mizrahi Jews,
whose ancestors were primarily from Spain, North Africa,
and the Middle East, and Ashkenazi Jews, whose ancestors
are primarily from Germany, Eastern Europe, and northern
France. Moreover, many Jewish people are also Black, living
in the United States, Ethiopia, and a number of other African
nations. There are also plenty of Indian Jews, Latinx Jews,
and Asian Jews. But no matter where they are from or what
they look like, history is full of violence against Jewish people
from all places. There were times that converting to another
religion could save a Jewish person's life and times when it
would not, because "Jewishness" was seen as part of that
person's essential nature.

Nazi Germany was an example of the latter. Its persecution of Jews was based on both racist nationalism and an
obsession with racist genetic pseudoscience. Although the
Nazis prioritized white supremacy and murdered other people
besides Jews, they reserved a special level of hatred for Jews.
They even argued that the Jews manipulated other, non-white
races in a campaign to "debase" white culture. One of Adolf
Hitler's many anti-Jewish rants in his 1925 manifesto *Mein
Kampf* claims,

> It was and is the Jews who bring the Negroes into the
> Rhineland, always with the same secret thought and
> clear aim of ruining the hated white race by the necessary
> resulting bastardization, throwing it down from its
> cultural and political height, and himself rising to be the
> master.
>
> For a racially pure people which is conscious of its
> blood can never be enslaved by the Jew. In this world he
> will forever be master over bastards and bastards alone.[10]

Unfortunately, this myth didn't die out with the fall of Nazi Germany. You can see the direct line from Hitler's manifesto to the ideas espoused by contemporary white supremacists, who believe that Jews are behind an intricate plan for "white genocide." Robert Bowers, one of the terrorists we mentioned at the beginning of the chapter, repeated the same paranoid antisemitism when he murdered 11 Jewish people in a synagogue in 2018 because he believed Jews were bringing refugees to the United States to wipe out white people.

Nazis believed that reviving medieval history—or perhaps, more accurately, pseudohistory since the Nazis waged an extensive campaign to rewrite Germany's medieval past—would restore white power. They thought the medieval past held buried Germanic glory, and that returning to the masculine models of medieval Germanic heroes would motivate Germans to purge the nation of non-Aryan races.

The Nazi neomedieval campaign was meant to inspire confidence in, and loyalty to, the Third Reich by invoking a sanitized, all-white version of history and its heroes. As Laurie A. Finke and Martin B. Shichtman first explored in their 2004 book *King Arthur and the Myth of History*, Nazis promoted Arthurian legends, and knighthood in general, as their own foundational myths.[11] The Third Reich created portraits—both rhetorical and artistic—of Nazi elites as chivalric knights. They even created "Order Castles," schools for party officials that were intended to model medieval knightly orders. And there's a reason cinematic heroes like Captain America and Indiana Jones always find Nazis trying to dig up relics from medieval legends: the Third Reich was obsessed with the medieval occult. Heinrich Himmler, commander of the Nazi SS, even funded expeditions to find the Holy Grail.

Nazi neomedieval identity hinged on a revisionist historical project in which they enlisted an army of literature and folklore scholars, archaeologists, historians, and linguists. These scholars were tasked with linking the stories, faith, and traditions of all the cultures Nazis admired to Germanic myth and folklore, and creating historical and linguistic "evidence" that German culture was supreme in human history. When these scholars could not find any connections, they invented them, arguing that links between Aryan cultures had decayed because of "foreign elements." The goal of this historical revision was to prove the existence of an Aryan race from which Germans could claim descent, and to exterminate all the cultural elements they thought of as foreign. Ultimately, and tragically, this included the *people* they deemed foreign too.

For instance, Himmler founded the *Ahnenerbe*, a Nazi "research institute" that was part of the SS. It was comprised of historians and other scholars devoted to the task of inventing a prehistoric pan-Germanic past, with or without the cooperation of the facts. Nazi archaeologists worked to uncover any scrap of evidence they could to support their totalizing worldview of "Aryanism." In 1937, they funded an archaeological expedition to Val Camonica, in the Italian Alps; the historian they sent there claimed that he found Norse runes among the prehistoric inscriptions (*note: he did not find anything of the sort*). The Nazis took this as evidence that the Norse had founded Ancient Rome (*note: they did not do anything of the sort*).[12]

The early twentieth century saw a whole movement of "Ariosophy" (meaning, roughly, "the Wisdom of the Aryans")—a field of people interested in the supposed ancient Germanic wisdom being uncovered by the Nazis and their predecessors. Ariosophists saw mystical meanings and magical powers in Norse runes and hidden symbolism everywhere. Nazis seeking hidden wisdom could be found staring intently at the frames of old wooden houses, desperately trying to figure out what secret messages were encoded within them.

Folklore was also extremely important to the Nazi revision of history. As folklore scholar Christa Kamenetsky explains, Nazis claimed that the suppression of Nordic folklore had led to the "decline of the West," and by restoring that medieval wisdom, they could save Germany from "cultural decay."[13]

So, they enlisted folklore scholars to provide evidence for links between the more domestic Germanic folklore recorded by the Brothers Grimm and the somewhat grander, heroic Norse and Icelandic legends. This led to some pretty wild comparisons: the doves seen in Grimm's fairy tales transformed into Odin's ravens; the German Cinderella was reinterpreted as Gudrun—Siegfried's wife. Little Red Riding Hood was really the primeval Norse mother, a symbol of fertility.

Unfortunately, as outlandish as all this "research" sounds, it influenced popular common knowledge. Few people understood what was going on behind the scenes in the academy or in German universities until decades afterwards. This means that much of the research done around the time of the Third Reich accidentally utilizes the Nazis' revisionist treatment of folklore, myth, and medieval legend. And some of this work is in the public domain—uncritically cited on *Wikipedia*, free on Google Books, and circulated on some blogs—whereas the more up-to-date research is often hidden behind an academic paywall or in expensive scholarly monographs. This deluge of free misinformation makes researching medieval legends extremely confusing for students and for the public. Without a clear understanding of the origin of a particular idea, it's easy to get taken in. And in the worst-case scenarios, you can see the inheritance of Nazi historical revisionism in the rhetoric and imagery that inspires today's white supremacist terrorists: the *sonnenrad* (sun wheel) that Nazi leader Heinrich Himmler used to decorate his castle, a symbol Nazi folklorists attributed to medieval "Germanic" cultures, was on the cover of the Christchurch terrorist's manifesto and on his ammunition bag.

The Nazis are often viewed as a horrific historical exception but the truth is, not only did their views and their medievalism have roots in the nationalism we discussed in the previous chapter but their fantasy of Aryan superiority was common in the Western world throughout the early twentieth century. Even in the United States, "Anglo-Saxon"

Protestant heritage was (and, by many white supremacists, still is) considered superior, which meant that along with horrific discrimination, Black Americans, Jews, Muslims, and Asian, Irish, and Italian immigrants (the latter two now usually considered white) were barred from certain restaurants and jobs, were more likely to be accused of crimes thanks to junk racial "science" like phrenology and Social Darwinism, and were subject to mob violence. Limits were placed on how many non-"Anglo-Saxon" immigrants were allowed in the country, which led to boats full of Jews being sent back to die in concentration camps during World War II. It wasn't easy to separate religious discrimination from racism in this era: Jews were mocked with ethnic stereotypes, Irish and Italians were considered inferior because they were Catholic, and Arabs were exoticized and mistrusted because of both their religion and their race.

A MODERN CRUSADE

IT WAS in this climate of early twentieth-century "Anglo-Saxon" self-aggrandizement that the Crusades surged back into the popular imagination. Pro-war propaganda against Muslim nations often invokes the Crusades and casts them as part of a greater cosmic struggle between good and evil. This is done to justify the horrors of war and to excuse the atrocities committed by one's own side. It allows those fighting in the conflict to feel righteous, as if they are God's own warriors. This violent propaganda reveals serious misconceptions about the past: that the Crusades were "holy," that the soldiers who fought in them were heroes or martyrs, and, most insidious of all, that the Crusades were somehow inevitable, part of an unending clash of civilizations between the Christian West and the Muslim Middle East. You might recognize this as the rhetoric around modern warfare in Afghanistan and Iraq, but in fact, it is at least as old as World War I.

A key example of Crusades rhetoric can be found in the fighting over the Sinai Peninsula and the region of Palestine during World War I. On one side was a coalition of Arab revolutionaries and their British allies, and on the other were the allied forces of Germany and the Ottoman Empire. The presence of the Ottomans in this fight provided easy fuel for World War I-as-crusade propaganda for the British. In fact, that propaganda was so prevalent that the British Press Bureau had to release a D-notice (essentially, a request to censor a story for military security reasons) to the press on 15 November 1917 that read:

> The attention of the Press is again drawn to the undesirability of publishing any article, paragraph, or picture suggesting that military operations against Turkey are in any sense a Holy War, a modern Crusade, or have anything whatsoever to do with religious questions. The British Empire is said to contain a hundred million Mohammedan subjects of the King and it is obviously mischievous to suggest that our quarrel with Turkey is one between Christianity and Islam.[14]

The press were not the only ones to blame for the medieval rhetoric: some members of the British military also seemed to believe they were on a holy crusade. Edmund Allenby, the leader of the British Empire's Egyptian Expeditionary Force, captured Jerusalem from the Ottomans on 9 December 1917. Despite the censorship notice put out by the Press Bureau, the influential magazine *Punch* published a cartoon (see Figure 3.1) in which the spirit of Richard the Lionheart personally approved of the conquest.

One of Allenby's subordinates, Major Vivian Gilbert, published a book in 1923 entitled *The Romance of the Last Crusade: With Allenby to Jerusalem*, in which he wrote: "of the ten crusades organised and equipped to free the Holy City, only two of them were really successful,—the first under Godfrey de Bouillon and the last under Edmund Allenby."[15]

FIGURE 3.1 "The Last Crusade," in *Punch, or the London Charivari*, 19 December 1917, p. 415. Obtained from Project Gutenberg: https://archive.org/details/punchvol152a153lemouoft/page/n889.

Gilbert viewed the war through a very common lens: that the "Holy Land"—or any place that, according to his mind, should be ruled by Christians—is "unfree" and in need of liberation when it is ruled by Muslims. Other British writers made the same medieval references, writing books about the battle for Jerusalem with titles like *The Modern Crusaders* (1920), *The Last Crusade* (1940), and *With Allenby's Crusaders* (1923).[16]

After World War I, as European nations broke up the Ottoman Empire, divided its territory among themselves, and invaded and colonized the Middle East, the memory of the Crusades returned. Some Europeans saw themselves as conquering crusaders, like French General Henri Gourand who said, upon conquering Damascus, "Behold, Saladin, we have returned."[17] Thus, it seems only fair that Middle Eastern leaders eventually began to envision themselves as those who *resisted* the Christian crusaders. In the post-WWII period, as the nations of Syria, Egypt, Lebanon, Iraq, and others fought for and achieved their independence, their nationalist movements looked to the Middle Ages for inspiration and focused, as Gourand did, on the highly mythologized medieval figure of "Saladin."

The historical warrior Salah ad-Din Yusuf Ibn Ayyub was important to both Muslim and Christian writers of the Middle Ages. Muslim historians like Bahā ad-Dīn, who knew Saladin personally, praise him as a just, valorous, and generous ruler, and make particular note of his humble devotion to Islam. But others, like Ibn al-Athir, were less positive: they blamed Saladin for destroying the Zengid Dynasty in Syria— a particularly scathing accusation since the Zengid hero Nur ad-Din had been especially successful against European invaders. Saladin was an entirely different character in medieval European poetry, but not always an antagonist. The brave, chivalric "Saracen" knight starred in multiple heroic poems about the Third Crusade, portrayed as the noble opponent of Richard the Lionheart. But in order to make Saladin more palatable to medieval Christian audiences, he had to be more Christian himself. In several medieval French poems, including the thirteenth-century *L'Ordene de Chevalerie*, Saladin is knighted by his French prisoner, Sir Hugh de Tabarie. He is called "saintly" in the fourteenth-century medieval Dutch poem *The Book of Vengeance*, and in the French *Le pas Saladin*, he travels around Europe with his buddy Hugh to learn all about Christianity.

This chivalric, Christianized Saladin became an appealing figure for nineteenth-century British medieval enthusiasts. In 1825, Sir Walter Scott published *The Talisman*, a novel set during the Crusades, which solidified and popularized Saladin's myth for a new generation. But Saladin was resurrected in the Muslim world too: in 1878 the Ottoman Empire restored Saladin's tomb and promoted him as a hero. In the mid-twentieth century, as nations like Egypt and Syria struggled for their independence from England and France, Saladin was reclaimed as an anti-Western figurehead, an avatar of opposition to European, American, and emerging Israeli power.

This resulted in a surge of historical and cultural adaptations of Saladin's life as his legend grew. Egyptian filmmaker Youssef Chahine made a big-budget film (financed by the Egyptian state) called *El Naser Salahadin*, which equated Saladin to Egyptian President Gamal Nasser.[18] Nasser also frequently referred to the medieval hero in his speeches.[19] But Nasser's approach was different from many contemporary leaders in the region—he promoted a pan-Arab nationalism that was based on uniting the Arab world across both its national *and* its religious lines, embracing, for example, Egypt's significant Arab-Christian and Jewish minorities. Leaders like Iraq's Saddam Hussein and Syria's Hafaz al-Assad also believed they were inheriting Saladin's legacy: al-Assad erected a massive statue of Saladin in downtown Damascus, and Hussein commissioned murals, statues, and even a children's book that likened him to Saladin.[20]

These associations between contemporary conflicts and the Crusades were repeated in the media and became part of the popular historical consciousness of conflicts between Middle Eastern and Western governments. At that point, both sides were manipulating medieval history to stoke international conflict.

MEDIEVAL 9/11

In 1993, American political scientist Samuel P. Huntington published in *Foreign Affairs* what would become his most popular and most controversial article: "The Clash of Civilizations?", which he expanded into a book in 1996.[21] Huntington argued that the world was split into civilizations defined chiefly by religion and culture: "Western," Orthodox, Islamic, Buddhist, Hindu, etc. He proposed that each of these civilizations had such different values that they couldn't help but come into conflict. "The fault lines between civilizations," he warned, "will be the battle lines of the future."[22] It's a vastly oversimplified view of world cultures, political history, and people. It does not give much credence to cultural exchange, genuine multiculturalism, or humanistic values. But his ideas gained traction after 11 September 2001, because Huntington saw "Islamic" civilization as one destined for conflict with the "Western" world.

It's worth noting at this point that "culture" in Huntington's theory functions as a kind of code word—you can tell by his long list of religions that are practiced in predominantly non-white countries, interrupted only by reference to a seemingly theologically neutral "Western" identity. His formula became particularly appealing to white Americans and Europeans in the post-9/11 world, when the shock of the attack on the World Trade Center in New York City provoked a wave of Islamophobia that was almost always conflated with racism.

At the turn of the new century, the Islamophobia that spread like wildfire in the wake of the attack fueled cries for a new crusade—and thanks to the internet and 24-hour news, this time it echoed on a massive scale. Both Osama bin Laden and the United States under the presidency of George W. Bush invoked the Crusades in the ensuing wars in Iraq and Afghanistan. Two weeks after the 11 September 2001 attacks, President George W. Bush said in a speech on the White House lawn, "This is a new kind of—a new kind of evil. And we understand. And the American people are beginning to understand. This *crusade*, this war on terrorism is going to take a while. And the American people must be patient. I'm going to be patient."[23] In the days that followed Bush's speech, White House staff attempted to walk back the statement, because when Bush used the word *crusade*, he seemed to be confirming what bin Laden and others like him had preached for years: that no matter its stated intentions, the United States was conducting a war not just on a specific group of radicals, but on all Muslims.

According to bin Laden, the US was not interested in dismantling terrorist organizations, but in conquest. It was motivated not by a desire for justified retaliation, but by religious hatred. He believed the US was conducting a crusade in the medieval sense, not in the bland aspirational sense. Bin Laden had been using the word *crusader* to refer to many of his opponents, including Israel and America, for years. For example, in his 1996 "Declaration of War against the Americans Occupying the Land of the Two Holy Places," he said: "It should not be hidden from you that the people of Islam had suffered from aggression, iniquity and injustice imposed on them by the Zionist-Crusaders alliance and their collaborators."[24] Two years later, he issued another statement titled "Jihad Against Jews and Crusaders," within which he railed against "the Crusader-Zionist alliance."[25] It was through this lens that bin Laden saw many of the world's conflicts: the Israeli-Palestinian conflict, the American wars in Iraq and Afghanistan, the UN's condemnation of his actions, and even conflicts between India and Pakistan. All of it was part of a grand Crusader-Zionist effort against Islam.

Bin Laden's rhetoric fundamentally divided the world into two groups: jihadis and crusaders. For the vast majority of Muslims, the word *jihad* is simply the internal, everyday spiritual struggle to be a better person. But radicals like bin Laden seized on the term and used it to mean something violent. The Western media hasn't helped, often further equating *jihad* with violence in their audience's minds.

As the war in Iraq drew on, the shame of Bush's comparison wore off. American conservative media began to root enthusiastically for military intervention in the Middle East by conjuring up their own vision of a medieval holy war. James Pinkerton, Fox News pundit, praised the invasion of the Middle East as part of a "crusader spirit" in 2003, arguing that, like the medieval Crusades, the war was "about bringing civilization and salvation of a backward people."[26] The real medieval Crusades, however, were never about "bringing civilization" to anyone, since by most accounts medieval

Muslims were more culturally and technologically advanced than medieval Christians.

The wars in Iraq and Afghanistan have gone on for nearly two decades as of the writing of this book, and although Huntington's theory has been dismissed by numerous scholars, a few continue to embrace it, such as historian Niall Ferguson, who writes books with titles like *Civilization: The West and the Rest* (2011) and headlines documentaries like *Civilization: Is the West History?* (2011).[27] Unfortunately, scholars like Ferguson are particularly influential, in part because their ideas resonate with far-right conservative politicians and others who hope to profit from continued war.

Western supremacists like Huntington and his intellectual descendants take the position that "The West"—which is typically only a more-acceptable way of saying "the majority-white parts of the world"—is superior, either due to what they imagine are its inherent sociological characteristics or based upon its history. Those who embrace this idea may not consider themselves racists, but the medievalism inherent in their project, in which they paint non-Western cultures as "medieval," "barbaric," and "backwards" in an effort to argue for how dangerous they are, is a very sheer veil for prejudice.

CIVILIZATIONAL CONSERVATIVES

This same toxic cocktail of white supremacy, antisemitism, and Islamophobia dominates the latest pseudointellectual incarnation of Huntington's theory, known as "civilizational conservatism."[28] Peter Beinart, writing for *The Atlantic* in 2016, coined the term *civilizational conservative* to describe a growing right-wing political force that is willing to cast democracy aside to ensure white Christian supremacy.[29] Allied with the so-called alt-right, civilizational conservatives believe in restoring a "medieval" world via violent conquest.

They often invoke the Crusades, but what they really want is a neomedieval race war, one they are working hard to bring to fruition.

Steve Bannon, Trump's former chief strategist and one of the authors of the Muslim travel ban in the United States, is the most infamous civilizational conservative in modern politics. Bannon believes that Christians are already in a "global war against Islamic fascism," and in a 2014 speech at the Vatican, he cited the Crusades as a model for action:

> If you look back at the long history of the Judeo-Christian West's struggle against Islam, I believe that our forefathers kept their stance, and I think they did the right thing. I think they kept it out of the world, whether it was at Vienna, or Tours, or other places.... It bequeathed to us the great institution that is the church of the West.[30]

Bannon's speeches and activism are augmented by his film-making career, which includes a documentary film called *Torchbearer*, starring *Duck Dynasty*'s Phil Robertson, that uses gruesome, violent imagery to argue that forming a "Judeo-Christian republic" is the only way to save Western civilization.[31]

Civilizational conservatives love to pay lip service to Israel, but antisemitism is always a companion to their Islamophobia. Despite his supposed championship of "Judeo-Christian" ideals, Bannon is the same man who allegedly did not want his daughters going to school with Jews.[32] He gives speeches full of antisemitic dog whistles, including bashing the "corporatist, global media," and "cosmopolitanism," both of which translate as "Jewish" in the white-supremacist ear.[33]

The extremist evangelical contingent of civilizational conservatism believes that Jews should to go back to Israel because of a prophecy that Christ will return during a civilizational war in the Middle East. At the end of this war, the "twelve tribes" of Israel will convert and usher in the Second

Coming. In order to have their longed-for Armageddon, these fanatics need the Jews to stay alive—and in Israel—for their eventual conversion. This apocalyptic theory is behind Trump's declaration of Jerusalem as the capital of Israel.[34]

The Russian interference in America's 2016 election also has links to medievalism, antisemitism, and Islamophobia. White supremacists, both in shady online venues like the neo-Nazi website *Stormfront* and on mainstream television like Fox News, have long touted Russia, and Vladimir Putin, as the last great bastions of white civilization. Never mind that Russia is technically in the east—Putin fans believe he is destined to defend the west. White supremacists who populate the message boards at the neo-Nazi website *Daily Stormer* laud Putin's attempt to raise the white birth rate in his country and praise the fact that his regime is causing Jews to leave Russia. Alt-right leader Richard Spencer, who celebrated Trump's electoral win by leading a room full of people in a Nazi salute, praised Putin's Russia as the "sole white power in the world."[35] And it isn't just extreme white supremacists writing love letters to Putin: Bryan Fischer, spokesman for the fundamentalist American Family Association, called Putin the "lion of Christianity," and Pat Buchanan wrote a 2013 article for *The American Conservative* urging his fellow conservatives to consider embracing the Russian leader: "In the culture war for mankind's future, is he one of us?"[36]

In November 2016, anti-terrorist intelligence specialist Malcolm Nance warned in an interview on MSNBC that the Trump administration's embrace of Russia was linked to white nationalism and possible plans for war in the Middle East: "What we're seeing is an alignment where people believe that they have to align the United States and Russia as an axis of Christendom against Islam, in a clash of civilizations that Osama bin Laden dreamed about."[37] Nance even predicted— long before the white-supremacist terrorist attacks in the US began—that we would see more mass atrocities committed by white supremacist neo-crusaders like Anders Breivik in

Norway. Unfortunately, Nance has turned out to be absolutely right.

The internet helped white supremacists eager to stoke anti-semitism and Islamophobia, spreading their ideas further and faster than at any point in history. Even since the first draft of this book, the violence continues to grow. In April 2019, John T. Earnest attacked a California synagogue, murdering one woman and injuring others, and tried to livestream the attack on Facebook. He claimed that the Christchurch killer's manifesto, which he found online, inspired his terrorism. Earnest's manifesto railed against Jews who he claimed, just as Hitler had, were using immigrants and Black people to destroy the white race.

Earnest's attack on the synagogue shows the way that Nazi ideas, once forcefully rejected by America and Europe, have been revived, spreading like a contagion across the web. And if medieval and modern history teach us anything, it is how these ideas can move rapidly from endangering innocent people in one mosque or one synagogue to wiping out the Jewish or Muslim population of an entire city or country.

MEDIEVAL MODELS OF HATE

THOSE WHO view the Crusades as aspirational or who think that Christian and Muslim civilizations are destined to be locked in an unending struggle would have you believe that medieval Christians, Muslims, and Jews were in a constant state of war.[38] But although religious violence was a feature of the medieval world, it was far from the whole story. Medieval interfaith communities thrived, and people of different faiths learned from each other, even in the face of persecution and invasion. We want to be cautious in this section: to record the roots of modern antisemitism and Islamophobia that were planted in the Middle Ages, but also to show how rich and active medieval cultural exchange could be and how people of multiple faiths not only survived in the Middle Ages but thrived.

Notoriously, anti-Jewish violence was rampant throughout medieval Europe. Many medieval European kingdoms kept Jews isolated and oppressed. Life for Jews could be unpredictable, and shifts in leadership, or hatred stoked by the Crusades, could turn deadly. Jews in England, France, and Germany were often limited in their professions: they were sometimes allowed to serve as moneylenders, since Christians were forbidden from doing it. Jewish people were sometimes employed by medieval kings to collect taxes and debts when those kings needed money but personally wanted to avoid the prohibition against usury. This not only led to resentment from borrowers, it also fed the stereotype that Jewish power came from manipulating money. In 1190, for instance, the use of Jews as debt collectors led to anti-Jewish riots in York in which the city's entire Jewish population was massacred.

Jews became a convenient scapegoat for any leader who wanted to increase his political power or get himself out of trouble, and many rulers made statements by "cracking down" on Jews or expelling them. Philip II of France—in debt at the ripe old age of 15—kidnapped Jews and held them for ransom, then confiscated Jewish property and expelled them from France. He allowed Jews to return in 1198 but imposed heavy taxes on them. The Fourth Lateran Council in the early 1200s worsened this kind of antisemitism, and its companion Islamophobia, by making an official statement that Jews didn't really "belong" in Christian countries. The council decreed that Jews could not hold public office or appear in public on certain holy days, and that both Jews *and* Muslims had to be marked by special clothing to set them apart so that they didn't mix with Christian women—particularly in the "biblical" sense. Edward I exiled Jews from England in 1290. In 1306, Philip IV of France arrested 100,000 Jews, seized their property, and expelled them on the grounds that they represented a state within a state, a charge of Jewish disloyalty that echoes to this day, with President Trump recently making that accusation against Jews who vote for Democrats.[39] French Jews were invited back by Philip's successor, who found that when his own agents tried to collect debts, the people didn't like them so much either; Jews would be banished from France and then readmitted in repeated cycles for nearly 200 years.

Paranoid fantasies about Jews stoked by religious and political leaders resulted in violence all over Europe. In the mid-1300s, Jews were even accused of causing the Black Death, and they were slaughtered throughout Switzerland and Germany because of it. And the Middle Ages saw the birth of the "blood libel" conspiracy theory that accused Jews of using the blood of Christian children in religious rituals. Though it has absolutely no basis in reality, enough medieval people believed it that several unsolved murders of children were blamed on local Jewish communities, which led to widespread anti-Jewish violence.

Life may have reinforced art, and vice versa, in much of Europe. Even medieval Christian writers who are known for some degree of tolerance toward other faiths—like John Mandeville, whose narrator concludes that Christians and Muslims have much in common—exhibits a paranoid fear and loathing of Jews. *Mandeville's Travels* repeatedly asserts that Jews are "wicked" and claims that many Jews are enclosed between the Scythian hills, but at the time of the antichrist, they will emerge to destroy Christians.[40] Jews were frequently the villains of medieval horror stories, like Chaucer's infamous Prioress's tale, in which Jews murder an innocent child and cast him into a pit "in the same place where these Jews purge their entrails."[41] Popular Passion plays, which traveled from town to town recreating the torment and crucifixion of Christ, regularly whipped up anti-Jewish fervor.

The Crusades pitted Christians against Muslims and Jews alike. But although white Christian supremacists like to glorify the Crusades as part of an inevitable Muslim/Christian holy war, the truth is that medieval crusades were often launched against people of multiple faiths, including other Christians; sometimes these were for political reasons, or sometimes they were simple land-grabs. For instance, the infamous slogan "Kill them all and let God sort them out"—something contemporary Islamophobes use to stoke violence against Muslims—was allegedly the instruction when soldiers took the city of Béziers in France during Pope Innocent III's crusade against the Cathar Christian heresy.[42] The crusaders massacred the entire city. Crusaders also attacked Al-Andalus to seize territory from Muslims and launched violent efforts to convert pagans in the Baltics.

Even though they weren't the only targets of crusader violence, Muslims and Jews both suffered from these attacks, whether they were in territories invaded by crusaders or in towns where crusade fervor sparked pogroms. Eliezer bar Nathan's twelfth-century Hebrew chronicle, *Persecutions of 1096*, recounts a massacre of Jews at Mainz inspired by crusader sentiment: "The enemy rose against them, killing little children and women, youth and old men, viciously—all in one day."[43] But some contemporaneous Christian writers condemned these murders. Albrecht of Achen's twelfth-century *History of the Journey to Jerusalem* describes the 1096 massacre by saying Christians "rose up in a spirit of cruelty against the Jewish people throughout these cities and slaughtered them without mercy."[44] Twelfth-century chronicler William of Newburgh recounts the York massacre of 1190 with sorrow eight years later, saying,

> The zeal of the Christians against the Jews in England ... was not indeed sincere, that is, solely for the sake of the faith, but in rivalry for the luck of others from envy of their good fortune. Bold and greedy men thought that they were doing an act pleasing to God, while they robbed or destroyed rebels against Christ and carried out the work of their own cupidity with savage joy and without any, or only the slightest, scruple of conscience.[45]

Even French literature meant to celebrate victories in the Crusades mixes admiration for crusading heroes with horror, even if horror in the reader may be an unintentional consequence of their accounts. *Richard Coer de Lyon*, a fourteenth-century Middle English romance that recounts the exploits of the famous hero Richard the Lionheart, details Richard cannibalizing his Muslim victims during the Third Crusade. Chroniclers also document Christian cannibalism during the First Crusade.[46] Raymond d'Aguilers, who traveled with the crusaders, notes in his twelfth-century account of the First Crusade on Jerusalem that the invaders "had taken many Saracen castles and villages and forced the Saracens to work, as though they were their serfs."[47] He praises the Saracens for their mechanical ingenuity, their fortitude in battle, and their perseverance, even as he calls the gruesome ending the "judgement of God": "Piles of heads, hands, and feet were to be seen in the streets of the city. It was necessary to pick one's way over the bodies of men and horses."[48]

Writers today talk about "the Crusades" as one coherent ideological phenomenon, but medieval Muslim writers would not recognize the grand narrative spun by Christian propagandists. Instead, they experienced what we call "the Crusades" as a series of invasions, or as senseless, random violence committed not just against their fellow Muslims but also against Christians. On their way to Constantinople in 1096, "the Franj," as Muslim writers called the French crusaders, raided and burned Christian farms and tortured Orthodox priests.[49] Muslim writers remember the "Franj" as cruel, foolish, and barbaric: there are tales of crusaders destroying cities in search of relics and treasure, and of cannibalizing Muslims. Usāma Ibn Munqidh, a twelfth-century Syrian poet, saw the Christian invaders as "beasts superior in courage and fighting ardour but in nothing else, just as animals are superior in strength and aggression."[50] Other times, Muslim writers simply seem irritated by the constant traffic of crusaders through their countries. Twelfth-century poet Ibn Sārah of Santarem gently mocked them in his poem "Pool with Turtles":

> Now they squabble on the bank
> but when winter comes
> they'll dive below and hide.
> At play they resemble
> Christian soldiers
> wearing on their backs
> their leather shields.[51]

AN INTERFAITH MEDIEVAL WORLD

As you can see, history paints a grim picture of both Jewish life in medieval Europe and Christian wars against Muslims. But although you might be more accustomed to hearing about the medieval history of religious wars and extremism, the average medieval Jewish or Muslim person would have experienced life very differently, particularly in interfaith communities where Christians, Muslims, and Jews lived side by side.

The violent discrimination against Jews in places like England and France did not reflect the rest of the world's attitudes and practices, not even in the rest of Europe, where plenty of medieval Jews pursued science, literature, and the arts. In southern Europe, which was diverse, cosmopolitan, and innovative, Spanish and Italian Jews thrived alongside Muslims and Christians for centuries. Jews also populated the medieval Middle East, where tolerance by Muslim rulers of other monotheists (like Jews and Christians) was generally the norm. For much of the Middle Ages, the metropolis of Baghdad was the center of the Jewish world. As scholar Robert Chazan recounts,

> the Jews of the realm of Islam in its heyday (c. 800–c. 1100) were by no means regular victims of mob violence,

religious persecution, or exploitation by the ruling class.
The Jews of the Islamic sphere grew in numbers, flourished
economically, interacted vigorously with their creative
non-Jewish milieu, fashioned major institutions of Jewish
intellectual and spiritual activity, and produced great
intellectual and spiritual leaders and works.[52]

The Muslim-ruled section of the Iberian peninsula, known
by its Arabic name, Al-Andalus, was a thriving center of interfaith art, literature, philosophy, science, and medicine and a
center of relative religious tolerance. We stress the word *relative* here, since there can be a tendency to describe Al-Andalus
either as a "Golden Age" of perfect religious harmony or a
dark age of violent religious persecution. But although modern people often see medieval culture in unrealistic, black-
and-white terms, neither the utopic nor dystopic vision of
Al-Andalus's past is completely true.

Many Andalusian Jews flourished intellectually and profes-
sionally. Famous figures include Judah ibn Tibbon, "father
of translators," Abraham Ibn Ezra, whose work ranged
from biblical commentary to mathematics and astrology,
and Maimonides, one of the medieval world's most influential
scholars. The ruling class in Al-Andalus was Muslim, but Jews
could be, and were, promoted to posts as high as vizier—the
key advisor to a Muslim ruler. Samuel HaNagid, for instance,
was a Jewish general in the Muslim king's army. Jewish poets
also exchanged literary influences with Muslim writers; there's
a clear record of exchange between Andalusian poets and the
rest of medieval Europe.[53]

As the political and cultural winds shifted, however, Jews in
southern Europe were also subject to raids and mass murders,
especially when fanatical religious movements attempted to
wipe out difference and dissent. For instance, when the more
orthodox Muslim Almohad movement invaded Al-Andalus near
the end of the twelfth century, it overturned the previous ruler's
policy of religious tolerance and forced Jews and Christians
to convert to Islam. Many of those Jews who refused fled to
Rome. Jews also found themselves in the middle of violent

clashes between Christians and Muslims during the Crusades, and later, during repeated Christian efforts to conquer Iberia (the peninsula that includes modern-day Spain and Portugal).

Unfortunately, as southern Europe became more religiously homogenous, whether Muslim or Christian, it became a more hazardous place for Jews. A rising tide of anti-Jewish hatred, massacres, and mass conversions in the fourteenth century lay the groundwork for the Inquisition launched by Christian rulers Ferdinand and Isabella. As the Middle Ages drew to a close, the Jews were expelled from Spain in 1492, when Christians conquered the remaining Muslim regions. Spain officially welcomed Sephardic Jews back in 2012, offering Spanish citizenship to those whose ancestors were driven out at the end of the Middle Ages.[54]

In other parts of Europe, although there was little tolerance for Jews, Muslims had a more mixed reception. Some medieval Christian literature exhibited Islamophobia, but some also exhibited curiosity and even admiration, casting "Saracen" knights and "Moorish" princesses as courtly heroes and heroines. Nameless "Saracens"—a word that could sometimes mean "pagan" but was mostly associated with Arabic Muslims—were the enemies in many romances, and Crusades poetry often gloried in their slaughter. Dante's *Inferno* places Mohammad in the eighth circle of hell, among the sowers of scandal and schism, who are split down the middle and tear open their own chests.

However, other medieval writers noted the similarities between Muslims and Christians. We mentioned Mandeville earlier, and while he may have been fervently antisemitic, his opinions on Muslims were relatively enlightened. In *The Booke of John Mandeville* (commonly known as *Mandeville's Travels*) during the narrator's fictional dialogue with the sultan of Egypt, Muslims are revealed to have a lot in common with Christians, including many shared beliefs, except that Muslims are even more devout and honest. The sultan accuses Christians of pride, gluttony, and all manner of shallow covetousness: "they are so proud that they don't even know what to wear: sometimes long clothes, sometimes short clothes, sometimes straight, and sometimes wide," and "they are so covetous, that for a little silver they will sell their wife, child, and sister. And men take other men's wives, and no man will keep his faith with another."[55] The Christian narrator seems to agree with the sultan and hopes to bring his wisdom back to his fellow Christians.

Muslim characters also star as heroic knights in medieval romances or as noble damsels living in courts imagined as parallels to Christian kingdoms. Saladin, the same historical figure resurrected in the nineteenth century, appeared in many medieval romances; so did the Saracen Arthurian knight Sir Palomides, who follows the Questing Beast, and his two brothers. (Later versions like Sir Thomas Malory's *Le Morte d'Arthur* has Palomides and his brothers convert to Christianity, but in earlier legends, they remain Muslim.) Saracen women are portrayed as love objects or even heroines in French and English literature, but only if or because they convert to Christianity: Josian, Bevis of Hampton's wife, is one heroic example. Floripas, a sultan's daughter who appears alongside her knightly brother Fierebras in multiple French and English poems, turns against her father to side with Christian knights and eventually converts. In the fifteenth-century *Sultan of Babylon*, Floripas even pushes her own governess out a window and kills a jailer to protect the knights.

These literary examples of interfaith dialogue and romance are imperfect at best, racist and Islamophobic at their worst. As depressingly intolerant as it is that in many medieval minds, the only good Muslim was one who converts, it does show that medieval religious discrimination wasn't racialized in exactly the same way Islamophobia is today. (The roots of this racism do exist in medieval literature, something we'll discuss more in the following chapter.) Most important to keep in mind, however, is that there was no one way of relating among faiths in the medieval world. The medieval world was not a monolith. Medieval kingdoms and empires fought against their co-religionists far more often than they fought kingdoms led by other faiths. There was also significant travel, migration, and diversity, especially in major centers of commerce and in the borderlands between kingdoms, empires, and nations. Members of different medieval faiths coexisted in the same cities and towns throughout most of their lives.

Finally, there was nothing uniquely medieval about the religious violence that happened in the Middle Ages. The persecution of Jews began in the ancient world and continued throughout the Renaissance, driven both by the Inquisition in Catholic countries and by Martin Luther's own antisemitism in Protestant nations. Anti-Jewish violence persists throughout the world today, even after the tragedy of the Holocaust. The Inquisition also attacked and forcibly converted Muslims well into the Renaissance. Christians waged a centuries-long campaign to violently conquer, convert, and enslave Africa, the Middle East, and the Americas. The Muslim Ottoman Empire taxed and sometimes forcibly converted Christians. Throughout the world, since the medieval period, Islam, Christianity, Hinduism, Buddhism, and other faiths have clashed violently, not because of any particular cultural nature, or because of the nature of their time period, but because war is part of human nature. But, as the medieval period can teach us, so are coexistence, shared knowledge, and peace.

4

WHITE (SUPREMACIST) KNIGHTS

> Freeland was one of the real chivalry of the South; besides
> being himself a slaveholder, he was a horse-racer, cock-
> fighter, gambler, and, to crown the whole, an inveterate
> drunkard.
>
> —William Wells Brown, "Narrative of the Life
> and Escape of William Wells Brown," 1847[1]

IN OUR last chapter, we detailed the way history's most infamous white supremacists, the Nazis, had an obsession with
medievalism that led to horrific violence. But the Third Reich
had a model for wielding a fake Middle Ages as a weapon:
the American Ku Klux Klan. Hitler saw American racial
segregation—and what he called "the southern way"—as a
promising method for making Germany racially "pure." The
Klan used fantasies of an all-white medieval past to fuel its
propaganda and to cloak its violence in false heroism. In fact,
white supremacists have long used the Middle Ages to make
claims for their own greatness and as a weapon to be wielded
against anyone who isn't white.

What draws racists so strongly to the medieval past? In
part, this is due to the myth that the Middle Ages was a
predominantly white culture. It's easy to see where this idea
might come from. Medieval fantasy novels and films, if they
have non-white characters at all, often depict them as violent,
backwards, or even sub-human. The notoriously barbaric
portrayal of the Dothraki in the recent HBO series *Game
of Thrones* is one example, as are the clearly racialized evil
hordes attacking astride elephantine creatures in the *Lord
of the Rings* movies. But even the history books you read

in school probably focused exclusively on the European Middle Ages. Popular culture would have you believe that white, western Europeans were the most important people in the medieval world. But as you already suspect, they're absolutely wrong.

In this chapter, we'll take you through the centuries of propaganda that elevated medieval Europe, and medieval white people, in the modern imagination. We will show how this was done at the expense of real people in history, whose stories have been ignored, and we will illuminate the tragic, violent consequences that have come from this misrepresentation of the past.

MEDIEVALISM AND AMERICAN RACISM

THE AMERICAN South had a long love affair with medievalism throughout the antebellum period.[2] Southern slaveholders imagined themselves to be nobles conquering and ruling a "new land," and they created their own version of chivalry and courtly society. They whitewashed their murder and enslavement of Africans by imagining it as neomedieval feudalism and themselves as benevolent neomedieval lords ruling over grateful serfs. Southerners challenged each other to duels and jousted in tournaments for entertainment. They dreamed up bloodlines that connected them to medieval heroes and kings, and they commissioned medieval coats of arms to display in their homes. Sir Walter Scott's 1820 medieval-themed novel *Ivanhoe* became so wildly popular that southern white people reimagined their society in its image, something Mark Twain famously derided as "Sir Walter disease."[3]

After the South lost the Civil War, its attachment to medievalism grew even more fervent. Suddenly, southern white men had to compete with Black men politically and economically. The formerly enslaved people who had been forced to labor in white people's homes and on their plantations joined the workforce, ran for office, bought property, and grew crops for their own income instead of lining the pockets of their former masters.

Soon after Emancipation, Black writers and intellectuals were publishing histories, biographies, philosophy, and fiction. Freed slaves were starting businesses and families. Black teachers launched schools to educate the newly freed and to help each other build careers and lives. Black culture soared, enriching the southern states that had held it back for so long; by the late nineteenth century, over 2000 Black men held political office. For instance, in 1870, Hiram Rhodes Revels was elected to the US Senate, and Joseph Rainey was elected to the House of Representatives.

But some southern whites were angry about all this progress. They believed their medieval "heritage"—their supposed right to rule by virtue of their race—had been stolen from them. And they were determined to get it back.

We often imagine that social progress is linear—that as time goes on, things improve and societies become more tolerant, fair, and equitable. It's an optimistic idea. The problem is, it just isn't true. Social progress often goes hurtling backwards when people who once had all the power get angry about the changes they see around them. The years after the Civil War and Emancipation are a key example of a time when progress decidedly reversed course. And nostalgia for an imagined Middle Ages full of heroic white people made it worse. Southern white people turned to the medieval legends they were nursed on for solace and propagated a new fantasy of the medieval past to try to reclaim their power.

The vanguard of that fantasy was the "White Knights" of the Ku Klux Klan. There have been three distinct iterations of the Klan. The original Ku Klux Klan first donned their hoods just after the Civil War and used violent terrorism, political maneuvering, and medievalism in their attempt to halt Reconstruction and re-impose white supremacy on the South. Calling themselves "The Invisible Empire," Klan members fancied themselves knights and dressed in elaborate, theatrical costumes and masks to terrorize Black citizens. Though this original Klan was only active until 1871, it helped launch a violent backlash against Black progress. Klan members didn't just ride through the streets on a campaign of murder and terrorism—they seized official channels of power too, through voter suppression and intimidation. Once in power, they instituted the Jim Crow laws and other oppressive systems to take back the freedoms that Black Americans had just won. The legacy of the first Klan still lingers: a statue of its original "Grand Wizard," Nathan Bedford Forrest, looms over a major Tennessee highway to this day.

Most people are more familiar with the Klan's second incarnation, which formed in the early twentieth century, once white southerners had reinstated the social hierarchy they thought they deserved. The second Klan's medievalism was even more fervent than the first's: it was nostalgic for a chivalric antebellum South that never really existed, and it championed the first Klan as a knightly band of heroes who slew the twin dragons of racial equality and Reconstruction. In 1905, Thomas Dixon romanticized the terrorist actions of the first Ku Klux Klan as a story of neomedieval vengeance in his novel *The Clansman*. The book portrays Reconstruction as a kind of living hell for white people: former slaves have taken over and destroyed the government, the banks, and the police force, driving the South into violent chaos. But the last straw is the rape of a young white woman by a freed slave. Ben Cameron, who will become the Grand Dragon of Dixon's novel, uses the young woman's rape and her resulting suicide to mobilize white men into an "Institution of Chivalry," one that bands together for the sole purpose of violently protecting white women's virtue:

> In a land of light and beauty and love our women are prisoners of danger and fear. While the heathen walks his native heath unharmed and unafraid, in this fair Christian Southland our sisters, wives, and daughters dare not stroll at twilight through the streets or step beyond the highway at noon.[4]

The Grand Dragon's new "chivalric order" launches a campaign of violence, intimidation, and murder to force white supremacy back onto the South.

In his novel, Dixon creates medieval origin stories for many aspects of the Ku Klux Klan, including the burning cross that would be a hallmark of white terrorism in the twentieth century, which he calls "The Fiery Cross of old Scotland's hills."[5] (In reality, medieval people were, as a rule, not very positive at all about burning their crosses.) Dixon's narrator also gushes about his heroes' knightly appearances and their ancestry as the descendants of medieval Scots: "The moon was now shining brightly, and its light shimmering on the silent horses and men with their tall spiked caps made a picture such as the world had not seen since the Knights of the Middle Ages rode on their Holy Crusades."[6]

Dixon's book might have become just another relic of the old South if it hadn't been for director D.W. Griffith, who turned *The Clansman* into a film that would shake the United States to its core in 1915: *The Birth of a Nation* (see Figure 4.1). Thanks to Griffith's influential connections—President Woodrow Wilson, who had been friends with Dixon in college, screened *The Birth of a Nation* at the White House—Dixon's dream of white supremacist medievalism went mainstream, and countless Black Americans suffered and died because of his racist nostalgia. The Klan had already committed decades of terrorism against Black citizens. Now, thanks to the film, its ideology was even more appealing to white people. By 1925, millions of Americans had joined the Ku Klux Klan.

Medievalism supercharged the Klan's recruiting power, from its regalia and heraldry to its rhetoric of white knighthood and faux chivalry. In 1921, the Charlottesville Klan advertised for members by asking potential "knights": "can you take a MAN'S OATH?" A chilling preview of today's white supremacist talking points, the ad calls for "law and order" and promises "protection for the good and needy, especially for women," while announcing that the Ku Klux Klan is specifically seeking "native-born white Americans"

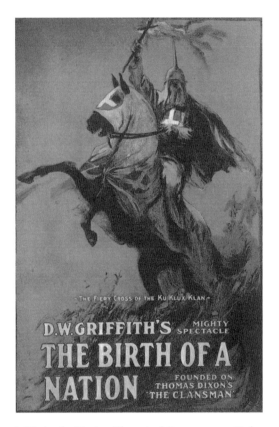

FIGURE 4.1 *Birth of a Nation* Theatrical Poster, 1915. Unknown artist. Obtained from https://commons.wikimedia.org/w/index.php?curid=10122298.

who believe in "Christian religion," "Free Speech," "Liberty," and "White Supremacy."[7]

These neomedieval fantasies about protecting white female bodies led to an epidemic of violence against Black Americans. Black men were punished for any relationship with white women, whether real or imagined. False accusations against one man could turn into violence against whole Black communities: white people with delusions of heroism formed lynch mobs in Omaha, Nebraska; they massacred families in Rosewood, Florida; and they decimated an entire Black business district in Tulsa, Oklahoma. And these are only the most famous examples.

Klan-led violence against Black citizens was both rampant and ruthless, and it continues to this day. If you don't live in or travel to the American South, you would be forgiven for thinking that the Ku Klux Klan's ghostly riders have faded into the mists of time. But they're still there, they're still angry, and they still have far too much power. The second Klan was dissolved by the 1940s, at least in an official capacity. The third Klan, the one that still exists today, rose up in the 1950s as part of the backlash against civil rights. This latest iteration of the Ku Klux Klan is diffuse: it consists of a patchwork of independent local groups that each take the name and mission of the Ku Klux Klan. In 2017, the Southern Poverty Law Center (SPLC) estimated that there are "at least 29 separate, rival Klan groups currently active in the United States."[8]

Though the Klan's membership is far from its 1920s peak, its influence is still keenly felt. For example, in February 2019, Goodloe Sutton, editor of an Alabama newspaper, declared that the "Klan needs to ride again" to raid the communities of Democrats who wanted to raise taxes in Alabama.[9] "Democrats," in southern conservative parlance, is thinly veiled code for both Black voters and the diverse politicians who are winning at the ballot box all over the country. The Ku Klux Klan still regularly papers neighborhoods with recruitment flyers and is highly active online. And Klan rhetoric and Klan members still promote violence: David Duke, former Grand Wizard of the Ku Klux Klan, is regularly interviewed on television and radio, and has over 50,000 followers on Twitter. In 2015, Dylann Roof cited the Klan's twisted "chivalric" white male anxiety about white female bodies when he murdered nine Black Americans who had welcomed him into their Wednesday night Bible study in Charleston, South Carolina. "You rape our women and you're taking over our country," he told them. "You have to go."[10] After the massacre, the Ku Klux Klan papered neighborhoods with celebratory flyers and red-and-white-striped candies.

The Ku Klux Klan may have gone underground to some extent in the twenty-first century, but its ideas have gone global. The Klan began recruiting efforts as far north as Canada in 2016, with flyers that read "Loyal White Knights of the Ku Klux Klan! Yes! White Lives Do Matter!" and "We Must Secure the Existence of Our People & A Future for White Children" (the latter slogan is known as the "Fourteen Words," used by hate groups and racist mass murderers to signal their allegiance to white supremacy).[11] The Klan has also permeated online spaces, from blatant hate sites like *Stormfront* to social media and message boards like 8chan, Reddit, and even YouTube, Twitter, and Facebook. Racists use the internet to spread their ideas, to organize violent rallies, and to incite murder.

RACISM GOES DIGITAL

THE KLAN isn't the only hate group using the internet to spread its poison. Online, global hate groups have converged, finding common ground in both racism and medievalism. Hate groups today have names soaked in medievalism like "Wolves of Vinland," "Rebel Brigade Knights of the True Invisible Empire," "The Holy Nation of Odin," as well as the enduring "Loyal White Knights of the Ku Klux Klan." The "Soldiers of Odin" attack migrants in Sweden and Finland while pretending they're patrolling the streets. The "Proud Boys" even formed their own neomedieval militia: they call it "The Fraternal Order of Alt Knights" (FOAK).[12]

At violent white nationalist riots in Charlottesville, Virginia, and Berkeley, California, in 2017 and 2018, members of the crowds wore crusader and Templar symbols. The Charlottesville hate groups alternately chanted "You will not replace us!" and "Jews will not replace us!"[13] The "great replacement" theory, a clear descendent of the Nazi belief that white people will soon be out-populated thanks to immigration, has metastasized online and even become common among right-wing media pundits and politicians. It also has deadly consequences, such as the August 2019 massacre in El Paso, Texas, in which the killer railed against a supposed white genocide and murdered 22 people, specifically targeting Mexican immigrants.

White supremacist groups are also joining forces because online culture gives them ample ground for sharing ideas and plans. The "Unite the Right" riot at Charlottesville in 2017 made it especially clear how much groups that had previously seemed distinct—neo-Nazis and neo-Confederates, for instance—had been collaborating in online spaces. Ostensibly rallying around the proposed removal of a Robert E. Lee statue from a park in Charlottesville, white supremacist groups used the event to showcase their collective strength and present themselves as a neomedieval conquering army. They used chat rooms to teach each other how to march with shields, they discuss the historicity of symbols like Thor's hammer on message boards, and they recruited each other for race riots by posting pictures of themselves in chainmail on social media. Once they showed up in Charlottesville, they waved medieval banners, wore armor festooned with medieval symbols, and wielded swords and shields.[14] And Charlottesville was no mere performance: 32-year-old Heather Heyer was murdered when one of the neo-Nazis attacked her with his car. White supremacists injured others as well, including DeAndre Harris, who was beaten with pipes by six neo-Nazis.[15]

Neomedieval conspiracy theories and pseudo-philosophies also run wild online, radicalizing white people in less obvious ways. One example is the "Dark Enlightenment," an internet-born theory that claims all modern problems started at the end of the Middle Ages. According to Dark Enlightenment proponents, humanism, democracy, and the quest for equality are responsible for the decay of Western civilization. Dark Enlightenment fans contrast the diversity of modern times with a mythological view of the Middle Ages as the height of white greatness, a time when every race was in its "proper" *geo-graphical* place, allowing white civilization to thrive in supposedly glorious isolation. Suffice it to say, this is complete nonsense. As you've already read in these pages, there was no such thing as the homogenous, insular medieval Europe they hope to resurrect. But realism is not their strong suit: some of them even argue that democracy will lead to a literal zombie apocalypse, and that the only way to prevent this is to return to medieval monarchy.

Now, we know we've been harping on the ways that the medieval world has gotten short shrift in modern rhetoric, but even *we* wouldn't go to this extreme. No matter how rich, diverse, or interesting medievalists think the Middle Ages may have been, nobody wants our future to look like our past—especially if it's the twisted version of the past that lives in a racist's imagination.

NEOMEDIEVAL WHITE FEMINISM

ALTHOUGH THERE's very often a strong correlation between racism and sexism, that doesn't mean some white women aren't eager to jump on the white supremacist bandwagon, especially when it elevates their own sense of privilege. Plenty of women-centered online spaces fester with racism, and women often serve as mascots and cheerleaders of today's digital white supremacist movements.

Historically, white women have been portrayed as victims in need of protection by white supremacist men. But many women have not only been complicit in racist violence, they've encouraged it. Groups like the United Daughters of the Confederacy supported the Klan in the early twentieth century and helped build the confederate monuments we're still fighting about today; in their publication *The Southern Magazine*, they published screeds (many written by men) that called the Ku Klux Klan "the bravest and best men of the South," and argued in their August-September

1936 issue that Klan violence was necessary to protect white womanhood:

> Over this once happy land there hung a horrifying dread. The South was in the clutches of a veritable "Black Death," for every morn, it seemed, brought news of another outrage upon white womanhood.... What would you have done, men of the North? Would you have arisen, in spite of laws, in spite of Federal troops, in spite of impending imprisonment and possible death, in defense of a mother, a sister, a wife or a sweetheart? There can be but one answer, for manhood still lives, the blood is red, and the hearts are pure.[16]

This mythology of Black violence against white women led to the mass murder of Black men and obscured the very real epidemic of white violence against Black women, which white men could—and in many cases, still can—commit with impunity.

Medievalist racism also allowed white women to imagine *themselves* as warriors. Young women across the South adopted medieval names and regalia for their own rituals. The "Women of the Ku Klux Klan" formed just after women won suffrage and soon gained more than half a million members, complete with matching neomedieval regalia and invocations of Joan of Arc. We still live with these women's legacies today, from the confederate statues that inspire far-right riots to many modern sorority rituals. As recently as 2017, Wesleyan College—a women's college in Georgia—confessed that its class symbols and ceremonies had started when early twentieth-century students wanted to express their allegiance to the Ku Klux Klan. The class names carried their racist lineage in names like "the Tri-K Pirates" and "the Green Knights" until the college finally ended the practice in 2018.[17]

Today's digital neomedieval white supremacy movement has its own female leaders and cheerleaders. As a recent exposé by Seward Darby reveals, the alt-right's self-styled "Valkyries" are a major force in normalizing and mainstreaming the current radical, racist movement. In an interview with

Darby, alt-right leader Lana Lokteff claims that women's support was behind the rise of both Hitler and Trump. Lokteff uses medievalism to praise both herself and the white supremacist women she organizes, claiming they are all "lionesses and shield maidens and Valkyries" who can "inspire men to fight political battles for the future of white civilization."[18]

Alexandra Minna Stern's book *Proud Boys and the White Ethnostate* traces an alt-right "white baby challenge" led by women who, at first glance, appear to be harmless Instagram homesteader moms, brewing their own kombucha and growing organic vegetables.[19] These women are happy to embrace the submissive homemaker roles they imagine existed in some mythical all-white medieval past. They teach their YouTube viewers and Twitter followers from-scratch recipes alongside encouragement to "restore" a white pagan past and have as many white babies as possible. You might be surprised that so many women are willing to submit to "traditional" gender roles in the name of white patriarchy, but they are caught up in their own racist fantasies, imagining themselves as princesses and Valkyries standing beside their warrior men. That neomedieval appeal is just as effective for some white women as it was in the 1940s, when Hitler used it in his propaganda posters.

SCHOLARS FIGHT BACK

THE WAVE of current digital white supremacist medievalism has inspired a corresponding wave of scholarly pushback, with medievalists taking to digital media themselves to correct the record. Medievalists have long studied the connection between medievalism and white supremacy in their scholarship. As far back as the 1980s, scholars like Morton W. Bloomfield and Eugene D. Genovese were reflecting on the ways southern American slaveholders indulged in a fantasy of neomedieval "feudalism" to justify slavery and racism.[20] In the early 2000s, Laurie A. Finke and Martin B. Shichtman wrote a series of books investigating the importance of the Middle Ages to Nazi Germany and other fascist and white supremacist movements. Within the last ten years, scholars such as Daniel Wollenberg, Louise D'Arcens, Andrew B.R. Elliott, Cord Whittaker, Helen Young, and Matthew Vernon have published books on everything from racism in medieval-themed video games to the neomedieval motivations of white supremacist terrorists.[21]

Until recently, few academics took this analysis outside the ivory tower. But because of the rising tide of white supremacy and its tendency to adopt medieval symbolism, scholars have felt more urgently that they shouldn't just speak to each other about these issues: they should also be speaking to the public. In 2017, just before the inauguration of Donald Trump, the online magazine *The Public Medievalist* launched a series on "Race, Racism, and the Middle Ages" that served as a way for scholars to reach out to the public to explain that the Middle Ages weren't an all-white world, and to chronicle the dangerous white supremacist movements that spread misinformation about the past and use medievalism to try to justify horrific acts of violence.[22] Many medievalists have also reached out in the mainstream media, contributing to mass outlets like *The Washington Post's* "Made by History" column and the Australian news site *The Conversation*. Medieval historian-turned-journalist David Perry has published deep-dives of medievalism and white supremacy for CNN and *Pacific Standard*, Matthew Gabriele has chronicled the abuse of medieval history for *Forbes*, and Dorothy Kim traced white supremacist obsessions with Vikings for *Time*.[23] Scholars have even launched social media accounts like "People of Color in European Art History" (originally known as "Medieval POC"), devoted solely to chronicling the diversity of medieval and Renaissance Europe.[24] We've made links to all these articles and more available on the website for this book.[25]

Scholars like Sierra Lomuto, Adam Miyashiro, and Mary Rambaran-Olm are also leading important conversations about how to identify and dismantle white supremacy in university classrooms and in academia itself on websites like *In the (Medieval) Middle* and *Medievalists of Color*, and are organizing academic conferences and journal issues, to discuss these pressing problems.[26] After all, the myth of the all-white Middle Ages didn't just emerge out of thin air: it came from decades of textbooks that only talked about white Christians, from classrooms confined to a narrow canon of medieval literature like *Beowulf* and *Sir Gawain and the Green Knight*, from scholars knowingly or unknowingly perpetuating a white supremacist worldview, and from the lack of diversity in university faculty.

A classroom isn't just a space for talking about the past. It's a space that can change minds and hearts in the present. Take, for instance, the story of Derek Black. Derek Black was born into a family with deep roots in overt white supremacy: his father was Don Black, the founder of the neo-Nazi website *Stormfront*. David Duke, prominent white supremacist and white nationalist politician, is Derek's godfather. Clearly, Derek was groomed from an early age to take up the mantle as a leader of the American white supremacist movement.

But as Eli Saslow writes in *The Washington Post*, Derek was "outed" on his college campus as the scion of a prominent white supremacist family, which began his slow deradicalization. Derek credits this to, among other things, several courses he took in medieval studies, which taught him that the white supremacist histories he had been taught were lies:

> He learned that Western Europe had begun not as a great society of genetically superior people but as a technologically backward place that lagged behind Islamic culture. He studied the eighth century to the twelfth century, trying to trace back the modern concepts of race and whiteness, but he couldn't find them anywhere. "We basically just invented it," he concluded.[27]

Perhaps an equally significant part of the story is that Matthew Stephenson, one of the few Orthodox Jewish students on campus, invited Derek to a Friday evening Shabbat. Stephenson instructed his friends at the dinner that this "was not 'ambush Derek' time," that they were not there to shout at him.²⁸ Over the course of several months, and several such dinners, Derek began to open up and listen.

Teaching better histories and pushing back against white supremacists' warped ideas about the past is a crucial step in stripping racism of its supposed historical authority. We often talk about history as though it is purely objective and scientific, a series of facts that always receives a neutral reception. But ignoring the diversity of the medieval world—in textbooks, in classrooms, or even in popular culture—isn't just factually inaccurate. It's an omission with a white supremacist agenda, one that attempts to normalize the erasure of people of color from the past.

The white supremacists who marched on Charlottesville, who erect confederate monuments, who dress up like little boys playing knight with dangerous, grown-up weapons, profess a passion for all things medieval, but they really aren't interested in learning about history. Instead, they want to live in a fantasy world in which the most important and most powerful people look exactly like the image they see staring back at them in the mirror. And they want to rest of us to be forced to live in that world too.

THE DIVERSE MEDIEVAL WORLD

THE REAL medieval period was not a "whites only" apartheid world. It was not a fabled time of Aryan heroism, and Europe was not the center of the universe. As you already learned in Chapter Two, medieval Europeans were not the most learned, inventive, or worldly people in the Middle Ages, nor were they a homogenous culture isolated from the rest of the world.

Finding positive representations of people of color throughout medieval art and literature, even in places where people imagine that the only inhabitants were white, is relatively easy. The Egyptian Saint Maurice, celebrated throughout Germany, became the patron saint of the Holy Roman Empire and is clearly portrayed as African in medieval iconography, including in a thirteenth-century sculpture beside the grave of Otto I. The medieval author Bede recounts the history of Hadrian, an African diplomat and abbot who was instrumental to educating people about Christianity in England, in his *Ecclesiastical History of the English People*. People of color are common throughout medieval European art: you can find images of Black amazons in a fourteenth-century French painting and African and Middle-Eastern kings, knights, and merchants throughout illuminated manuscripts. Religious art meant to portray scenes from Christ's life is often particularly diverse. At least one—and sometimes all three—of the Magi will often be depicted as Black in medieval paintings.

German, French, and English medieval literature features plenty of non-white heroes and heroines. In the thirteenth-century German tale *Parzival*, written by Wolfram von Eschenbach, Parzival's Christian father falls in love with a Muslim woman, Belcane. Together, they have a child named Feirefiz, who winds up with variegated skin, black for his Muslim mother and white for his Christian father. Despite Wolfram's obvious confusion about how biology works, he explicitly states that Feirefiz was just as beautiful, wealthy, and strong as all the other knights. A magnificent warrior, aristocrat, and lover, it is only Feirefiz's faith that prevents him from seeing the Holy Grail until he converts to Christianity, but in every other way he is considered Parzival's equal—which is no small feat.

And Feirefiz was no aberration. The Black knight Sir Moriaen teams up with Lancelot and Gawain to find his father and rescue King Arthur in the fourteenth-century Middle Dutch romance *Moriaen*. French author Christine de Pizan lists African women in her defense of all womankind, *The Book of the City of Ladies*. She writes of Queen Zenobia, "The great courage of this lady and the chivalrous inclination she possessed were obvious throughout her childhood."[29] Both

Christine and Geoffrey Chaucer recount the tale of Dido, the queen of Carthage who was wooed and destroyed by the legendary Aeneas, with heartfelt pity. In *The Legend of Good Women,* Chaucer's narrator takes Dido's side, constantly calling her the "noble queen" and Aeneas "false."

Asian cultures have positive representations in European medieval literature as well—and with good reason. China was a thriving center of trade, literature, and the arts. Genghis Khan, leader of the Mongol Empire, made multiple cameos in French and English medieval literature and art. The most famous account is Marco Polo's travel to the court of Kublai Khan. "The Great Khan" was famous among medieval writers for his policy of religious tolerance, his interfaith court, and the wondrous inventions of his kingdom, which transcended the engineering capabilities of medieval Europe.

THE ROOTS OF MODERN RACISM

However, just as in modern literature, not all medieval representations of people of color are positive ones. Although many scholars were, until recently, reluctant to use modern terms like "racism" when discussing medieval people, and even though the categories medieval people used to define each other were different from our own, a few key medieval beliefs may well form the foundation of modern-day racism.[30]

The first belief was the way medieval people thought about the aristocracy. Medieval Europe was not a society with a whole lot of class mobility, mostly because that was the way the ruling class wanted it. Medieval nobles viewed themselves as a breed apart from the people they ruled—literally. They thought they had more in common with aristocrats in other kingdoms than with the "common" people of their own lands. And the aristocracy policed class borders through marriage, with particular emphasis on keeping their bloodlines "noble."

Romance, a medieval genre that celebrated the heroic deeds and love stories of very wealthy and powerful characters like kings, queens, knights, and ladies, constantly comments on the noble blood of its characters. Unsurprisingly, the nobility believed their blood carried traits that boosted their claims to superiority: they thought it made knights better warriors, women more modest and intelligent, and both men and women more attractive. Whiteness is also factored into class status in European medieval romance and was sometimes considered a symbol of noble birth, partly because nobles did not have to labor outdoors all day. Thus, the protagonist of the thirteenth-century romance *Silence*, a noble masquerading as a minstrel and living as a man despite being assigned female at birth, has to stain their glistening white skin with dye so that they will not reveal themself as royalty.

One common plot device in romance is a knight who disguises himself as a commoner but has his cover blown because he is *just so attractive*. Scholars call these the "Fair Unknown" romances, or *Bel Inconnu*, named after a popular medieval French tale in which a young man disguised by a fairy nevertheless realizes his "natural" inclination to become a knight. In Sir Thomas Malory's *Le Morte d'Arthur*, for instance, Gareth, brother of the famous Sir Gawain, comes to Arthur's court in disguise, hoping to earn his knighthood just like anyone else. But the moment he appears, everyone notices that he is "large and long and broad in the shoulders, well-visaged, and [had] the largest and the fairest hands that ever man did see."[31] Arthur declares that he should be treated like a "lord's son." Lancelot and Gawain even give him clothes and gold.

If you think this idea of "noble blood" giving a person extraordinary beauty, nobility, and strength is just a backwards medieval thing, you should note that it persists in some of our most enduring popular culture. Aragorn in *The Lord of the Rings* has the right to rule Gondor because of his ancestry, which also gives him extraordinary longevity. Modern versions of Arthurian legend keep the medieval trope that Arthur's noble blood allows him to pull the sword from the stone and rule England. Many of our most famous superheroes—Batman, Black Panther, Superman, Supergirl, Wonder Woman, Arrow, Iron Man—are either royalty in their own realms or members of the aristocracy. The question of Rey's parentage that consumed *Star Wars* fans since Episode VII's release focused exclusively on the Jedi, and when she seemed to have been sired by nobody in particular, some fans were outraged. Fan complaints may have contributed to J.J. Abrams's decision to reveal Rey to be a member of Jedi aristocracy in Episode IX; she spent much of that film struggling with the evil "in her blood."

A second medieval foundation of modern racism is something scholars call "geographical determinism." This is the theory that different environmental conditions—like the amount of sunlight and heat in a region, access to water, and temperature—could create different human capabilities and bodies. This biased theory is the one that Julius Caesar employed to argue that Rome had *the perfect* conditions for human flourishing. The ancient Roman claim to environmental perfection, though not quite what we would call racism, was obviously not ideologically neutral. It led to a skewed view of the rest of the world as somehow flawed and lumped people together based on physical appearance when their cultures were actually very distinct.

For instance, ancient Greeks and Romans used the term "Aetheopian" to incorrectly conflate the residents of sub-Egyptian Africa. The word comes from the Greek *Aethiops*, which may have meant "sunburnt" or "fiery-looking." But classical geographical determinism did not privilege whiteness. After all, ancient Romans were darker than Germanic tribes, whom the Romans considered strong and spirited because they bathed in cold rivers, but not particularly bright, because all that cold stifled the mind.

Medieval clerics, who often relied upon Roman texts, adopted the tendency to paint all of Africa with the broad "Aethiopian" brush. But because their nobility prized whiteness, they began to combine their geographical determinism with something that looked more like white supremacy. Bartholomaeus Anglicus, a thirteenth-century Franciscan monk, argued that the sun gave African men a darker complexion and curly hair, but because he thought courage could leak out of a man's pores, he claimed that Africans were "cowards." By contrast, men of the north (like Bartholomaeus himself, *of course*) were lucky enough to live in cold weather that "stoppeth the pores" and kept people "bolde and hardy."[32] Albertus Magnus argued in the thirteenth century that Indians were bound to be good at magic and mathematics because a little heat could make a person smarter, but he declared that Ethiopians would be incapable of such things because they are exposed to *too much* heat. These writers, just like ancient writers, were all happy to jump through whatever logical hoops were necessary in order to declare themselves the very best.

It's easy at this point to see how geographical determinism might transform into modern-day racism. But there is one important, additional factor that led us to modern racism: religion. Medieval people believed that bodies were vessels for souls, that souls could be "sick" because of spiritual conditions, and that those conditions could be diagnosed by looking at a person's body. An external change in appearance could be evidence of an emotional or religious problem. If a knight was looking pallid, he could be diagnosed with lovesickness. Leprosy was sometimes considered a physical manifestation of sin devouring the body, which led to the ostracization and abuse of people living with the disease.

Many medieval writers used this method of diagnosing a body to read meaning into the color of people's skin. Whiteness was often used as a metaphor for spiritual purity in aristocratic heroines, such as Chrétien de Troyes's Enide and Fenice, who are described as being white as lilies or with a bosom "more white than new-fallen snow."[33] Even in *Parzival*, Feirefiz's mother Belcane is abandoned by his Christian father, and she demonstrates her longing for him by constantly kissing her son's white spots.

Aristocratic hierarchy, geographical determinism, and religious beliefs all combined in the Middle Ages to create a way of thinking about cultures and bodies that was certainly a preview, if not an absolute equivalent, of modern racism. But there is one thing medieval people believed that we do not: over the course of generations, thirteenth-century German writer Albertus Magnus argued, people from Africa or the Middle East who were relocated to a cold climate would eventually turn white. In other words, Magnus, and many other medieval Europeans, believed that what we would call race today was changeable, not permanent. And that change was not always due to something as innocuous as geography. Sometimes, it was a matter of faith.

In the fourteenth-century English poem *The King of Tars*, race, faith, geography, and the myth of noble blood come together for a clear picture of how different strands of medieval racism prefigure modern white supremacy. *The King of Tars* features a Muslim sultan who converts to Christianity. At the moment of his conversion, his skin transforms from black to white. Worse yet is the poem's depiction of an interracial child. Before his conversion, the sultan has a son with his Christian wife, but that child is born a shapeless lump of flesh. He doesn't even have any bones. As soon as the child is baptized, however, he instantly transforms into a beautiful, healthy infant. The sultan's whiteness is a marker of his internal religious "purification," and his child isn't even considered human until he becomes a Christian. This medieval poet believed that a person's faith in the Christian God could help him "transcend" biology and birth.

The view of racial difference presented by *The King of Tars* certainly isn't better than modern racism. Arguably, in some ways, it is worse. But it is decidedly different. White supremacists will tell you that racism is somehow natural and constant throughout human history—just an example of human nature when we encounter someone who looks different from ourselves. But as you can see, this simply isn't true. Racism is an ideology that develops slowly over time, and that is often pushed by the wealthy and privileged. It's a social problem with roots we can very clearly trace.

However, the Middle Ages constituted a thousand years of history spanning continents and millions of people; there was not one Middle Ages, and as you have seen, these prejudices were far from universal, even in Europe. In more cosmopolitan medieval places like Al-Andalus, people interrogated racism. Thirteenth-century poet Ibn Sa'īd al-Maghribī, for instance, wove his social commentary into the poem "Black Horse with White Chest":

> Sons of Shem and Ham live harmoniously
> in him, and take no care for the words
> of would-be troublemakers.[34]

Even in today's supposedly enlightened scientific age, "would-be troublemakers" persist in looking for physical evidence of the condition of someone's soul and for their capabilities and inclinations. Too many people still believe that bodies function as prophetic tomes, texts we can read to determine a person's internal characteristics. But although the Middle Ages gave us a prototype for modern-day racism, they also gave us just as many examples of its opposite: dialogue, education, and diversity.

5

KNIGHTS IN SHINING ARMOR
AND DAMSELS IN DISTRESS

> For some—they are sometimes called the "optimists"—
> women's status is seen as having steadily improved ever
> since Europeans shrugged off the Middle Ages, woke up,
> bathed, and stopped grievously oppressing women.
> —Judith Bennett, *History Matters*, 2006[1]

GEORGE R.R. MARTIN'S *A Song of Ice and Fire* series—better
known as the popular television show *Game of Thrones*—is
famously considered "grimdark" fantasy, a genre which, when
set in a neomedieval world, invokes the dirty, brutal Middle
Ages of modern imagination. In other words, it's set in the
so-called Dark Ages. Gender oppression and people's beliefs
about gender in medieval times play an enormous role in making the world of Westeros feel more "realistic." In fact, when
questioned about the sexual violence and misogyny in his
books, Martin explained it away by saying, "I'm not writing
about contemporary sex. It's medieval."[2]

Many people are under the impression that life for medieval
women was radically different "back then," and that rape was
a defining part of the medieval world. Men were supposed to
have been brutal animals whose appetites were barely held in
check by chivalry, while women were helpless victims. Worse
yet, not everyone sees this as a problem: people who remain
wedded to strict gender definitions today often invoke the medieval period as a more authentic time, when men and women
were "hardwired" to behave in supposedly natural ways.

But medieval evidence doesn't conform to these gendered
assumptions. Knights in medieval literature wept, fainted,
and spent a lot of time being lovesick. Women wielded swords
and magic, rescued men, and argued philosophy and theology.

In real medieval life, women wrote stories and poems as well as scientific and medical treatises. Women writers, philosophers, and theologians also interrogated gender and defended each other. Most medieval cultures were patriarchal and privileged men—just like so many cultures throughout history and well into the present day. But medieval women still lived rich, fulfilling, and impressive lives.

Women's medieval achievements aren't the only thing rendered invisible by misinformed hindsight. Most people believed that medieval people were, for lack of a better term, completely heterosexual. But although same-sex desire was considered a sin by the Catholic Church, that certainly didn't stop everyone. Moreover, outside western Europe, same-sex desire was sometimes a tacitly or even openly accepted part of life. The same goes for transgender and nonbinary identities, which in the Middle Ages even had a religious aspect—some medieval saints were believed to have transcended gender altogether. The truth is that medieval people of all genders lived very much like we do today: negotiating their lives within and outside the rules and strictures used by family, faith, and other social structures to try to bind them.

THE CHIVALRIC RACKET

ONE OF the most intractable vestiges of medieval culture, and medievalism, is the myth of chivalry.[3] Most people think chivalry is relatively harmless, an old-fashioned idea of politeness that just means pulling out a chair or opening a car door. More fervent modern fans of chivalry are attracted to the "chivalric code" as an ideology of physical protection of the weak, fighting in someone else's defense, or as service to morality and faith. One thing almost everyone agrees on, however, is that chivalry is a masculine quality, something that only men can aspire to if they want to be "better."

However, there's a reason that feminist scholars call chivalry an age-old protection racket.[4] It's a concept that depends on men to protect women from male violence, and one that expects women to meet certain criteria in order to deserve protection—sort of like when the mafia leaves your restaurant alone because you pay them a bribe every month. And historically, the category of people who qualify as chivalric hasn't just been limited by gender—it has also been limited by race and class, most often considered the exclusive province of wealthy, white men. Ku Klux Klan members, as you learned in the previous chapter, declared themselves chivalric in their violent campaigns to keep white women from having relationships with Black men.

Chivalry has never prevented violence, not even in the Middle Ages. It only regulates certain kinds of violence against certain kinds of people. Twelfth-century French poet Chrétien de Troyes, famous for his chivalric romances, declared in *Lancelot* that if a noble woman were traveling alone, a knight could "no more treat her with dishonor than cut his own throat should a noble reputation concern him." But if he fought another knight for her, "he might do with her as he pleased without receiving censure or shame."[5] In Sir Thomas Malory's fifteenth-century *Le Morte d'Arthur*, the most influential medieval Arthurian legend (Mark Twain even called it his favorite book), Arthur's knights swear to protect upper-class women, but they also ignore sexual violence against peasants; sometimes that violence is even committed by those same knights.[6]

Because chivalry only values certain women, other women become targets. Men feel entitled to those unprotected bodies, and the crimes against them are considered mere "misbehavior." And just as chivalry only protects certain women, membership in the chivalric brotherhood is only available to certain men. In the Middle Ages, for instance, circular logic suggested that because only the highborn were capable of containing their violence, they were the only ones who should be trusted with it. In the thirteenth-century Old French *Lancelot-Grail*, the Lady of the Lake, who kidnaps Lancelot as a child so she can raise him, provides an exhaustive explanation of the symbolism behind all knightly accoutrements, from hauberk to shield to lance. But the horse is what symbolizes the aristocratic knight's relationship to the common people:

> The horse that the knight sits on and that takes him wherever he needs to go symbolizes the common people, for the people must likewise bear the knight and attend to his needs. The people must search out and provide him with everything he requires to live honorably, so that he may protect and defend them night and day. The knight sits astride the common people, for, just as the knight spurs his horse and guides it toward the goal he chooses, he has the task of guiding the people according to his will and in legitimate subjection; indeed, the people are under him, and that is where they are meant to be.[7]

You can see how this kind of attitude toward the people a knight is supposed to protect might lead to abuses of power. In fact, many medieval people themselves were highly suspicious of chivalric claims. In tale after medieval tale, chivalry either fails or is revealed to be an aristocratic charade. For instance, in Chaucer's *Wife of Bath's Tale*, an enchantress teaches a rapist knight, who thinks his noble blood and knightly station allow him to do whatever he wants, that true nobility comes from good acts, not aristocratic lineage: "Churlish sinful deeds make a churl," she tells him, and "Christ wants us to claim our nobility from him," not from "old richesse."[8] In medieval literature, courts of ladies often wind up having to judge knights for crimes against women. In Malory's *Le Morte d'Arthur*, Sir Gawain accidentally beheads a woman who throws herself in front of her knight to protect him. Lancelot's commitment to chivalry leads Elaine of Astolat to believe he loves her, but it's all a performance, and she commits suicide when he rejects her advances.

If these concepts of chivalry sound radically different from what *you* learned about chivalry, that's because our modern view of it developed in the nineteenth century, which tended to look back at the Middle Ages through a hazy lens that either ignored or simply edited out everything improper or offensive. (Scholars use the term *bowdlerized* to describe the way nineteenth-century translators cleaned up medieval texts, editing out the sex, blasphemy, and other naughty behavior.)[9] Writers like Sir Walter Scott imagined a chivalry that would inspire and prescribe masculine behavior—and which justified nineteenth-century gender roles, social mores, and international politics. Scott explains what he meant by chivalry in his famous 1819 novel *Ivanhoe*, when the title character is debating its merits with a female character:

> Chivalry!—why, maiden, she is the nurse of pure and high affection—the stay of the oppressed, the redresser of grievances, the curb of the power of the tyrant—Nobility were but an empty name without her, and liberty finds the best protection in her lance and her sword.[10]

You can, perhaps, see the transition the concept of chivalry went through between the Middle Ages and the height of nineteenth-century medievalism: Sir Walter Scott believed chivalry could "curb the power of the tyrant." But the medieval knight *was* the tyrant, riding astride the local commoners.

IT'S NOT A COMPLIMENT

CHIVALRY REQUIRES both passive women and violent men in order to justify its existence, and therefore, it reinforces a hierarchy that takes agency away from women. To put it plainly: strong, chivalrous men depend on passive women to let them be heroes. But you don't have to take our word for it: proponents of chivalry reveal this when they promote what they call a "complementary" definition of the sexes—a symbiotic relationship in which men and women have supposedly natural roles that support each other.[11] For instance, Brett McKay, author of the 2009 book *The Art of Manliness*, argues that chivalry "can foster mutual respect and remind us of our underlying biological differences and the complementary nature of the sexes. Some women will bear children, and some men will step up to be protectors should danger arise."[12]

To those who don't understand the full implications of his words, his thoughts may seem harmless or even natural. But the idea of complementary sexes as a natural phenomenon has been used by the worst proponents of medievalism to police gender roles. For instance, Nazi Minister of Propaganda Joseph Goebbels made nearly the same argument during a campaign to get women out of the workforce: "The mission of the woman is to be beautiful and to bring children into the world.... The female bird pretties herself for her mate and hatches the eggs for him. In exchange, the mate takes care of gathering the food, and stands guard and wards off the enemy."[13]

In fact, Nazis saw a complementary gender arrangement as a return to the authentic roles of their medieval "Aryan" ancestors. Hitler called on German women to stay home and nurture their children rather than "interfere" with the world of men, dismissing feminism as a "Jewish scheme."[14] Nazi posters featured their own soldiers drawn as knights to rally them to the battlefield, whereas their propaganda exhorting women to leave their jobs and nurture their children (and there was a lot of this propaganda) featured white women surrounded by blond children and nursing infants in a medieval-style Madonna-and-child pose, or women and children clustered beneath brave, shield-bearing husbands.

The theory that a strict gender binary is both "complementary" and medieval is still an essential part of white supremacist ideology today. Andrew Aglin, editor of the neo-Nazi news site *Daily Stormer*, made this statement on gender equality in 2015: "My position on women, very explicitly, is that they should in the modern world remain in the exact same role they were in during the medieval period and I am unwilling to dance around or negotiate on that issue. Women should be honored, cherished and cared for, but they should not possess 'rights.'"[15]

Complementary is a code word, whether Brett McKay realizes it or not. It means that one party gives up power to feed the power of another. One sex is valued for its strength and the other, for its vulnerability. Based on the theory of complementary genders, women need to step aside so that men can be strong—just the way we imagine medieval knights were.

Nazis, past and present, aren't the only ones who use the Middle Ages to push for women's submission to men. In the United States, some members of the mainstream Evangelical movement also champion this view. John Eldredge, author of a popular 2001 book on Christian masculinity entitled *Wild at Heart*, argues that reverting to medieval roles will save modern people's troubled relationships. Eldredge refers to women as "the Beauty" throughout his book, and he argues, "This world kills a woman's heart when it tells her to be tough, efficient, and independent ... her childish dreams of a knight in shining armor coming to rescue her are not girlish fantasies; they are the core of the feminine heart and the life she knows she was made for."[16]

Even though straight, cisgender men are highly privileged by neomedieval gender roles, the ideology behind them is also damaging to boys and men. Medievalism encourages men to believe that their violent inclinations are natural, healthy, and worth cultivating. For instance, Eldredge makes a point of eschewing any notion of a passive, loving Christ figure because that's just too wimpy: "Mr. Rogers with a beard. Telling me to be like him is like telling me to go limp and passive. I'd much rather be like William Wallace."[17] Meanwhile, William Wallace himself, and other medieval figures, would have been far more familiar with the medieval version of Christ, who was sometimes depicted nursing the faithful at his breast.

To Eldredge and other proponents of neomedieval complementary gender roles, male agency depends on having a woman to save: "What would Robin Hood or King Arthur be without the woman they love?"[18] Eldredge asks his reader, seemingly unaware that the medieval version of Robin Hood didn't have a girlfriend—his devotion to the Virgin Mary was revised to "Maid Marion" after the Middle Ages, when Catholicism lost favor—or that the woman King Arthur loved is famous for betraying him with his favorite knight and destroying his kingdom. As always, this kind of medievalism is revisionist history used to advance regressive goals. It is not based on any real interest in or knowledge of the Middle Ages.

FIGURE 5.1 *The Accolade*, painting by Edmund Leighton, 1901. Obtained from Wikimedia Commons: https://commons.wikimedia.org/wiki/File: Accolade_by_Edmund_Blair_Leighton_-_complete.jpg

Revisionist medievalism takes pains to put women in their places, sometimes literally. Take, for instance, *Sleeping Beauty and the Five Questions*, an instructional audio CD sold by the popular American Christian company Vision Forum in 2004. The CD's purpose is to teach fathers how to prepare their daughters to be submissive brides. Its cover features a doctored version of Edmund Leighton's famous 1901 painting *The Accolade*. Leighton's painting is of a young woman using a sword to knight a man who kneels before her (see Figure 5.1). But the Vision Forum CD cover adjusts *The Accolade*

FIGURE 5.2 *Sleeping Beauty and the Five Questions*, CD narrated by Douglas W. Phillips, 2004. Image obtained from visionfamilyforum. com's store page, now defunct.

by lifting up the man to hover over the woman and removing the sword from her hand (see Figure 5.2). (The CD's narrator, Doug Phillips, was sued for sexual harassment in 2014, and Vision Forum had to close down.)

The ill-informed "medieval" theory of complementary gender roles saturates modern extremist religious cultures, something we'll talk more about in the following chapter. But these ideas aren't exclusive to the radical fringe. Even in something as seemingly innocuous as LEGO—"Knight's Showdown" for boys, so they can imagine themselves at war, and "Rapunzel's Tower" for girls, so they can imagine themselves being rescued—neomedieval gender roles work to keep women and girls submissive so that men can shine.

Restrictive gender roles are a big enough problem. But the theory that two, interdependent, complementary genders are somehow historically natural also erases LGBTQ+ people completely, indoctrinating children into unnatural, ahistorical gender roles alongside heterosexism and self-loathing. Sometimes the anti-LGBTQ+ effects of this kind of medievalism are latent and ignorant, but sometimes, they're intentional. Gender "purists" use their warped view of the Middle Ages to rigidly police gender and sexuality and to enforce roles and relationships which, if they were as natural as these people claim, would not need to be enforced at all.

NEOMEDIEVAL RAPE CULTURE

THE MEDIEVALISM-INFUSED gender binary of passive, victimized women and heroic (or brutal) men normalizes sexual assault in modern culture. We mentioned the hit television show *Game of Thrones*, based on George R.R. Martin's *A Song of Ice and Fire* series, at the beginning of the chapter. Martin's novels are full of explicit sexual assaults, constant discussions and jokes about rape, and rape threats against female characters.[19] Nameless women are raped by raiding soldiers and warriors, rape is woven into national and familial histories in Westeros, and one particularly brutal rape results in a woman so traumatized that she is rendered mute. The words *rape*, *raped*, *raper*, *rapist*, or *raping* combined appear at least 171 times in Martin's books, and that's not including the other synonyms he uses to describe it.

No matter how grim *A Song of Ice and Fire's* view of medieval sex might be, though, the television show makes it worse. When Jaime Lannister and Brienne of Tarth, one of the only female knights in Westeros, are captured, Jaime says to her, "When we make camp for the night, you'll be raped, more than once. None of these fellows have ever been with a noble woman. You'd be wise not to resist…. If you fight them, they will kill you…. Let them have what they want. It doesn't matter."[20] Brienne asks him, "If you were a woman, you wouldn't resist? You'd let them do what they wanted?" "If I was a woman," Jaime replies, "I'd make them kill me. But I'm not, thank the Gods."

This conversation comes almost directly from the books; both text and television would have us believe that despite

Brienne being bigger, stronger, and better with her sword than Jaime, her womanhood makes her vulnerability inevitable. But HBO included two amplifying additions just to reinforce Brienne's vulnerability: "If you fight them, they'll kill you" is never uttered in the books, and it seems to indicate that if Brienne chose to "make them kill her" like Jaime would, she'd be classified as a victim, not a warrior. Second, and potentially more disturbing, is the added line, "none of these fellows have ever been with a noble woman," as though sexual assault is the same as "being with" someone, gang-raping a noble prisoner is as romantic as a tumble in the hay with the farmer's daughter.

The slippery continuum between sex and rape as well as the inevitability of female vulnerability also dictate the transformation of one of Martin's only erotic scenes into a brutal rape: Daenerys Targaryen and Khal Drogo's wedding night, which is consensual in the books. Moreover, in an entirely invented plotline for heroine Sansa Stark, the HBO show has her married to Ramsay Bolton—the Worst Person in Westeros—and he rapes her after their wedding night.

The showrunners for *Game of Thrones* defend the violent sexual assaults added into the television version of Westeros by claiming in a March 2017 interview with *The Daily Beast*, "It's not our world ... but it is a real world, and it's a violent world, a more brutal world.... It's a world where these horrible things are definitely pervasive elements of their lives and their cultures. We felt that shying away from these things would be doing a disservice to the reality and groundedness of George's vision."[21] Far too many people believe this version of the Middle Ages is authentic. Marital rape did happen in the Middle Ages. It's difficult to know how often. But it was not so common that every woman, or even most, went to their marital bed expecting violence. Marital rape also happens today. It was only criminalized in all 50 states in the USA in 1993—and only as a result of the concerted effort of feminists for nearly 150 years. And overall modern rape statistics are appalling: as a conservative estimate, one in six women in the

United States today have either been raped or are the survivor of an attempted rape, and women are still abducted into and raped in marriage around the world.[22]

The brutal world HBO created is, in many ways, more similar to our modern world. We have to own up to our own rape culture, not just displace it onto the past. It is the twenty-first century that brought the horrific rape of a two-year-old girl in India and the ten-year rape and captivity of three adolescent girls in Cleveland, Ohio. Ours is the world in which teenage boys videotape their crimes and tweet about them. And it is the twenty-first century, not the twelfth, in which US Senator Saxby Chambliss of Georgia explained the rate of sexual assault against women in the US military, one woman in three, by explaining, "The young folks that are coming into each of your services are anywhere from 17 to 22–23. Gee whiz—the hormone level created by nature sets in place the possibility for these types of things to occur."[23] And despite the fact that it is the twenty-first century, men who have been accused of rape still sit on the Supreme Court and in the White House.[24]

The almost exclusively female victims of sexual assault in *Game of Thrones*—and in the original books—also give lie to any claims of accuracy, historical or otherwise. Apart from oblique references to assault against boys, men are rarely vulnerable to rape in the faux-medieval world of Westeros. But war, hierarchical systems, and the cultural elevation of sexual dominance results in rampant sexual violence against men too. Between 21 per cent and 80 per cent of male political prisoners in Croatia, Iran, Kuwait, the former Soviet Union, Sarajevo, and the Congo reported being raped by their captors—and that's only what was reported.[25] The Pentagon estimates the rate of sexual assault against men in the United States military at 1.2 per cent, 38 men per day.[26] And notably, those figures are among soldiers; that doesn't count assaults against enemies or prisoners. Finally, the rape of men in prisons is so ubiquitous that it is commonly treated like a joke rather than a horrific crime.

We don't have reliable statistical analysis of sexual violence against medieval women or men. Like marital rape or the rape of slaves, legal protection did not seem to exist for many male victims, although sodomy was a punishable offense. And yet, we do have some suggestion of sexual violence against men in literature, including many Norse *sennas* (boasting contests that preceded a fight) that accuse men of being ridden like mares or assaulted by superior warriors. We also have descriptions of the rape of men listed among the many atrocities committed during the Crusades. And yet, *this* aspect of the real, violent, and brutal world is not one to which those who revel in the authenticity of medieval rape would like to remain faithful. Clearly, when reality and fantasy come into conflict, it is the illusions that flatter our own ideas about gender that will win out over the complexities of history or human nature.

Fictional instances of violence against women are used as a shortcut to make medievalism seem authentic. But they also shape modern culture, and not just with the smug but false assurance that we are better than our past. People today look to history to verify and validate their own behavior. For those looking to explain rape culture, myths about the brutal, patriarchal, heterosexist Middle Ages provides "evidence" that this is humanity's natural state. Not only is this deadly for modern women but it aggravates the culture of shame surrounding sexual assault against men. "Why complain?" this view of history seems to ask anyone who hopes to change patriarchal culture. "The world has always been a man's world. Just be grateful you don't live *back then*." It's a grim view of women's lives and an even grimmer view of men themselves—so much so that turning to the real Middle Ages is almost a relief.

GENDER IN THE MEDIEVAL WORLD

DESPITE WHAT you may see on television, most medieval men were not violent, and most of them didn't fight in wars. Only a few wealthy men were knights, and even men in "Viking" culture were more likely to tend farms and fields than raid their neighbors. (Raids were the province of the upper class, who had slaves and serfs to tend their estates and farms while they were away.) Despite this, re-enactment groups have far more modern men pretending to be sword-wielding aristocrats than farmers, serfs, clerks, merchants, parsons, or hermits. When modern people talk nostalgically about "medieval men," they mean warrior-aristocrats. Few people want to admit how much their nostalgia for medieval gender roles is so heavily dependent on class or that if they were transported back to medieval times, they would more likely be farmers or servants than princesses and kings.

Moreover, medieval women were not sheltered princesses guarding their purity, even when they were nobles. (The chastity belt never existed in medieval times, and the only ones around now were joke or fetish items forged in the eighteenth and nineteenth centuries.) Medieval noblewomen and royalty had extensive influence, education, and power. Anna Komnene, a twelfth-century Byzantine princess, was also a physician and a historian who wrote the *Alexiad*, which chronicled the First Crusade. The Empress Matilda had to fight a civil war for England against her own cousin, Stephen of Blois. She lost, but she ensured that her son, Henry II, would take the throne when Stephen died. Eleanor of Aquitaine, Henry II's queen, joined the Second Crusade with a troop of ladies-in-waiting, ushered in a literary renaissance, and eventually joined her son in a revolt against her own husband. And these women are the tip of the iceberg, not exceptions to the rule.

It can be tempting to write off medieval women because of the "common knowledge" that they lived in a patriarchal society. Most people don't know about medieval women and their achievements because they haven't bothered to look— sometimes, that even includes teachers and scholars. There are enough medieval women writers, for instance, to fill several semesters worth of reading. Twelfth-century writer Marie de France engaged in a literary recovery project, translating the legends of the Bretons, a people who lived in what is now

Brittany in France. Multilingual and an extraordinary poet, Marie told tales like *Lanval*, which was so popular throughout the Middle Ages that it was even translated into Old Norse. She also translated over 102 fables and a number of saints' lives. Christine de Pizan wrote the *Book of the City of Ladies* in defense of women, as well as several other literary and historical works, including a biography of Charles V. Medieval Japan was home to a great many female writers, including poets like Shirome and Michitsuna no Haha in the tenth century, and Mursaki Shikibu, who wrote the world's first novel, *The Tale of Genji*, in the eleventh century. In fact, women wrote poetry and songs all over the medieval world, like the ninth-century Byzantine hymnist Kassia and Jórunn Skáldmær, a tenth-century Norwegian *skald* (the Norse word for bard). Ulayya bint al-Mahdī wrote love poetry in eighth-century Baghdad, and Khosrovidukht wrote in eighth-century Armenia. Medieval women such as Julian of Norwich, Catherine of Siena, and Marguerite Porete were also prolific religious writers.

Many medieval women were polymaths—writers, theologians, scientists, and physicians—like Hildegard of Bingen, Trota of Salerno, and Lubna of Córdoba, a poet and a mathematician in tenth-century Iberia. In China, Xue Tao, Yu Xuanji, and Li Ye wrote poetry in the Tang Dynasty, Madame Huarui and Wang Qinghui were poets and concubines, and Guan Daosheng was a twelfth-century poet and painter. Laylā bint Ṭarīf was a ninth-century Muslim warrior-poet—and she was not the only one. And there are many more medieval women writers who may exist if we stop assuming that "Anonymous" was a man.

Medieval women were also religious leaders and businesswomen and practiced other professions. Abbesses and nuns were extremely influential in both the Church and in politics. Women were doctors in the early Middle Ages before universities began to exclude them. Still, even in the late Middle Ages, whole villages would have died without midwives. They would have been naked without the clothes women wove, imported, and sold. They would have starved without women's crops. And they would have been a lot soberer, but a lot sadder, without the leagues of female brewers who supplied the medieval world's ale.

The Middle Ages were patriarchal, but patriarchy is a power structure that changes shape, and that ebbs and flows with other social and cultural developments. Its nature is different in different places and times. After all, we're talking about hundreds of years and an entire world full of people and customs. So, while it is important to acknowledge real medieval women's suffering and oppression, it's also important not to infantilize them, to imagine that they were always helpless, or to dismiss their contributions to the world. Medieval women were *half* the world, and their lives counted.

Although men were privileged in most medieval cultures, medieval masculinity was defined very differently than we imagine it today. In some ways, medieval men had a much broader range of emotional expression available to them than American men do now. And they are much more vulnerable than you might expect. Sir Thomas Malory's *Le Morte d'Arthur*, which is considered a manly book about man things—weapons, knights, and combat—contains plenty of examples. His Lancelot is in near constant danger of being raped. Typical episodes include one in which Lancelot, haplessly sleeping under an apple tree, is suddenly dragged back to the Castle Charyot by four lascivious queens who intend to coerce his sexual services on penalty of death: "Choose one of us to have as your lover," they demand, "or die in prison."[27] Lancelot is rescued from this fate, but his heroic savior is a damsel, not another knight. In another episode, Lancelot actually *is* raped. The perpetrator is Elaine of Corbin, whose nursemaid enchants her to look like Guinevere, then gets Lancelot drunk and leads him to Elaine's bed. The term *rape* may seem anachronistic for this episode, but we can still recognize the traumatic reaction Lancelot has after the assault: he jumps out a window, takes off into the woods, and runs around half-naked for two years.[28]

Lancelot is not the only vulnerable knight in medieval legend. Sir Alexander is kidnapped by Morgan le Fay, who captures him to "do her pleasure whenever she wants it." Alexander claims, "I would rather cut away my 'hangers' than do her any such pleasure!"[29] Alexander escapes with both his chastity and his masculinity intact, however, thanks to a damsel who rescues him from prison. Even King Arthur is trapped by a sorceress, Aunowre, who tries to seduce him with magic. He is rescued by another sorceress, Nynyve, who has already swooped in to save the king from a mantle that would have set him on fire, and who rescued him during his battle against the knight Accolon. You might wade into Arthurian legend expecting to find knights rescuing ladies from towers, and there are a few, but you'll also find a surprising number of ladies rescuing knights.

Women also rescue other women from sexual peril in medieval romance: Thessala, a doctor in Chrétien de Troyes' *Cligès*, saves the lady Fenice who is forced to marry her beloved's uncle. By slipping the uncle a magical potion, Thessala ensures that he will make love to his wife only in his dreams, never touching her in reality. Next, she gets Fenice out of her marriage by helping her fake her own death. Thessala even goes up against a pack of male doctors: three physicians from Salerno are sadistically torturing Fenice to see if she's really dead when Thessala rushes to her rescue with a crowd of more than a thousand ladies, who break down the door with axes and hammers and hurl the physicians out the windows.

The portrayal of gritty, filthy, brutal masculinity and passive, victimized femininity in the Middle Ages is a modern fantasy in more ways than one. Take, for instance, Vikings, often considered the manliest men of medieval times. Viking men didn't run around with bare chests—they wore tunics, hats, and colorful clothing with intricate patterns and ribbons. Medieval chronicle evidence, such as John of Wallingford's in 1220, described the Vikings as well-groomed, charming heartbreakers:

> They were—according to their country's customs—in
> the habit of combing their hair every day, to bathe every
> Saturday, to change their clothes frequently and to draw

attention to themselves by means of many such frivolous whims. In this way, they sieged the married women's virtue and persuaded the daughters of even noble men to become their mistresses.[30]

Viking men were also scrupulous groomers. Archaeologists have found tweezers, nail cleaners, ear cleaners, and toothpicks from the age of Viking raids. And men were not the only ones to wield a sword: archaeologists have also found the graves of women who may have been Viking warriors.

If you're surprised by this information about the supposedly übermasculine Vikings, it's because our gender stereotypes in the modern era are very different from medieval ones. Gender is far from stable—not just among individuals, but among cultures and throughout time. Stereotypes of women were very different too. Consider a thirteenth-century poem called *De Coniuge non Ducenda*, commonly known as "Gawain on Marriage" or "Against Marrying." Found in over 55 manuscripts—so we know it was popular—*De Coniuge* describes one gender as "wanton" and "lustful," pretending to go on pilgrimages so they can sneak out to brothels, reveling in "unchastity," "deceitful, jealous," and "full of pride."[31] Which gender do you think they're talking about?

Women, of course! Medieval people believed that women were earthier, less faithful, and needed far more sex than men. In fact, unlike the current medievalisms that try to reinforce female purity, innocence, and passivity, medieval women were thought to be more sexually aggressive by nature. Medieval medicine also thought women were naturally colder, more calculating, and more deceitful than men because of their different humors. However, this wasn't quite the feminist viewpoint you might think: the beliefs stemmed from patriarchal ownership of women. Men who had taken wives by force or as a business arrangement were constantly paranoid that their "property" would stray. They also thought women were less intelligent, less spiritual, and more like animals than like people.

What changed? When did we get the prevailing idea that women are naturally more chaste and virtuous than men are? Well, there has always been something of a class divide at work. In the Middle Ages, purity and chastity were reserved for highly aristocratic women and saints, who were thought to be able to transcend their "typical" female natures. But in the nineteenth century, white culture began to use "purity" to distinguish white women from everyone else. Racists argued that if white people themselves were more "evolved," which those racists fervently wanted to believe, that meant white women had transcended qualities as mundane as lust or other appetites. As depressing as all this is, it should teach you that even the gender stereotypes that seem the most "natural" are, in fact, socially constructed and highly dependent on power, cultural conditions, and political propaganda.

THE LGBTQ+ MIDDLE AGES

ALTHOUGH EVERYONE who uses medievalism to police gender behaves as though there were only two genders in the medieval world, and only one sexual orientation, history reveals that this is just another set of false assumptions about the Middle Ages. Medieval people had same-sex partners and desires, lived as a gender other than the one they were assigned at birth, and even disrupted or expanded the notion of gender altogether.

The concept of sexual orientation as identity is relatively modern. Medieval literature will speak to us about same-sex acts but not of identities themselves, which can make things murkier. But we have enough evidence to conclude that sexuality was a spectrum, like it is today. We can also extrapolate this from ancient cultures like Greece and Rome, where for over 12 centuries, sexuality was a spectrum, bisexuality was the norm, with people who were only attracted to same-sex partners or opposite-sex partners at either end of that spectrum.

Asexuality is, perhaps, the easiest orientation other than heterosexuality to find evidence for in the Middle Ages. Although some who joined monasteries and convents didn't do so by choice (and even if they did, they didn't always remain chaste), asexuality was not just a valid medieval lifestyle—it was seen as a holy calling. People could thrive by devoting themselves to theology, literature, science, teaching, or even politics by taking vows of chastity. Even if one didn't join the Church at a young age, asexuality could be adopted later in life. The most famous example is Margery Kempe, a medieval mystic who swore off sex after giving birth to 14 children because she had a vision from God. Margery didn't just abandon her family either: instead, she talked her husband into an asexual marriage.

Examples of other queer sexualities in the Middle Ages may not be as obvious, but even though medieval people didn't use the exact same language to discuss sexuality, we can still identify queer moments in the past. In Marie de France's twelfth-century romance *Lanval*, the hero angers Guinevere by refusing to be seduced by her, so she accuses him of "heresy": "People have often told me that you have no interest in women," she tells him. "You have fine-looking boys with whom you enjoy yourself."[32] Now, Guinevere is wrong about Lanval—he has a female fairy lover he isn't allowed to tell anyone about. But the episode shows you that medieval people thought sexuality was about behavior rather than identity. Likewise, Christian clerical texts mention lesbianism as acts, not identity, referring to a woman's "vice with a woman," "devilish ways," or "playing a male role."[33] Medieval Muslim cultures had specific terms for lesbian practice based on the Arabic words for *pounding* and *rubbing*.[34] Their medical texts showed some awareness that same-sex desire between women was inborn, though they blamed unbalanced humors. And not all medieval representations of same-sex desire were negative either. A tenth-century Arabic book whose title translates as *Encyclopedia of Pleasure* tells a love story about a Muslim woman and a Christian woman and claims their love was far stronger than that between man and wife.

People could not usually marry same-sex partners, but they often didn't have to. Men and women who "married the church" by joining monasteries and nunneries (and were not asexual) lived their whole lives in close proximity to people of the same sex. Medieval marriages frequently were pragmatic ventures—many people married for procreation, for help on the farm, or for political reasons—so quite a few people found love and desire outside of matrimonial bonds.

The acceptance of same-sex desire changed over the course of the Middle Ages, which grew less rather than more tolerant over time. The original Christian prohibition against same-sex relationships came not from any specific anti-gay biblical passages but from the ascetic tradition, which asked humanity to reject *all* pleasures of the flesh in favor of spiritual transcendence. The Apostle Paul, a medieval favorite, basically argues that you should have no sex at all—but if you absolutely must, you should at least get married and make babies. Thus, earlier medieval practice equated same-sex acts with sins like masturbation. In the later Middle Ages, as the Church cracked down on heresies and as the Inquisition spread, punishments became far more severe. And in the Muslim world, the *Encyclopedia of Pleasure* was eventually banned.

We have more concrete records, both literary and historical, of transgender and nonbinary medieval people. The Norse gods, despite having a certain caché among right-wingers because of the Nazis' love affair with Norse culture, had a range of sexualities and gender identities. Loki famously changes his biological sex: in *Gylfaginning*, he turns into a mare in order to seduce a giant's stallion and win a bet. As a result, Loki gives birth to Odin's eight-legged horse, Sleipnir.

One of the most modern-feeling romances to emerge from the European Middle Ages is the thirteenth-century French romance *Silence*, in which the title character is assigned female at birth but takes on the mantle of a male knight in order to retain their right to inheritance. There are several ways to read this text. You can read it as a transgender story—that Silence is a man the whole time and comes to accept his gender identity and expression over time. It can be read as a story of gender fluidity, where Silence adopts the gender expression they prefer. Or it can be read through as a woman adopting traditionally male dress and behavior in order to succeed within and disrupt the patriarchal structures around her. Each of these readings is a reasonable approach to the text.[35] By the time she is 12 years old, Silence can defeat all of her peers at jousting, wrestling, and skirmishing. At this point, she is visited by three allegorical figures: Nature, Nurture, and Reason. Nature lambasts the young knight: "You have no business going off into the forest, jousting, hunting, shooting off arrows. Desist from all of this! ... Go to a chamber and learn to sew!"[36] Just as Silence is about to be persuaded by Nature's rhetoric, words which the narrator notably labels *sofime*—false arguments intended to deceive—Nurture arrives, and she is furious. "I have completely dis-Natured her!" she declares, "She will always resist you!" Finally, Reason convinces Silence that taking up the habits of Nature would be almost as bad as killing herself. "You will never train for knighthood," she warns, and "you will lose your horse and chariot."[37] After listening to Reason, Silence "saw, in short, that a man's life was much better than that of a woman." "Indeed," she decides, "it would be too bad to step down when I'm on top.... Now, I am honored and valued.... I'm a disgrace if I want to be one of the women [now that] I have a mouth too hard for kisses and arms too rough for embraces."[38] Hence Nurture and Reason have succeeded in changing Silence's body as well as her mind.

What's important about the nature, nurture, and gender debate in *Silence* is that it shows evidence of a medieval recognition that gender can be fluid. Silence's behavior erases Nature—after all, she is so good at performing masculinity that she outfights all the other boys. Moreover, when Nature, Nurture, and Reason visit Silence, each one is portrayed as an *external* force to be obeyed at will, and all three are separate from what we now label "biological sex." Reason, who argues for remaining male, is considered a prized faculty in medieval theology, delivered to the individual from God to lead one to

His truth. If nature, nurture, reason, politics, physical activity, and even God take part in shaping *Silence*, it's possible that medieval ideas about what we call gender might be even more complex than our own.

Religion is also an important factor in medieval gender identity, and not always in the ways you might think. Some people who were born female dressed as monks, joined monasteries, and only had their biological sex discovered after their deaths, like Theodora of Alexandria, Marinos the monk, and Smaragdus of Alexandria. Until recently, many historians have labeled these people as "cross-dressing" or "disguised" saints, rather than acknowledging that medieval people may have had similar feelings and experiences as transgender, nonbinary, and genderqueer people today. And while we cannot say definitively how they saw themselves since what we know was written *about* them and not *by* them, the fact that they maintained their male identities until their death implies that this was more than a "disguise"—this was how they chose to live their lives.

Let it not be said, however, that the Middle Ages were especially enlightened about gender. The infamous case of Joan of Arc is a telling one. Joan was celebrated for taking up men's clothing, armor, and weapons to fight the English. But she was ultimately burned as a heretic for refusing to renounce dressing as a man. The Middle Ages were hardly an open-minded paradise of feminism and sexual openness. But don't be fooled by anyone who wants to pretend medieval people did not have the same range of desires, dreams, and identities that we do today.

6

MEDIEVALISM AND
RELIGIOUS EXTREMISM

The theologian may indulge the pleasing task of describing Religion as she descended from Heaven, arrayed in her native purity. A more melancholy duty is imposed on the historian. He must discover the inevitable mixture of error and corruption, which she contracted in a long residence upon earth, among a weak and degenerate race of beings.
—Edward Gibbon, *The History of the Decline and Fall of the Roman Empire*, 1776[1]

W HEN ISIS exploded onto the front pages of western media, pundits were in a rush to call their tactics "barbaric" and "medieval." Headlines like "The Return to Medievalism" in *Slate* and "The New Dark Ages: The Chilling Medieval Society ISIS Extremists Seek to Impose in Iraq" in *The Daily Express*, and statements such as that from Nick Clegg, then–deputy prime minister of the UK, that the UK upholds the rule of law, "unlike these barbaric, medieval types in ISIL," showed the eagerness of journalists and politicians to portray ISIS as a relic of the medieval past.[2] Behind these accusations was an assumption that both ISIS and the Middle Ages were brutal and backwards. Lurking behind *that* was a thinly veiled racism eager to accuse Muslim people of barbarism.

However, ISIS's medieval label came from two sources. Its leaders also embraced medievalism, though their motives differed from Western media outlets: the group claimed to be establishing a new caliphate. The medieval caliphates were Islamic empires that reached their height in the seventh, eighth, and ninth centuries, ruling over parts of the Middle East, Africa, and Europe. ISIS's goal was to bring the "medieval" caliphate back, not only through violent conquest but through fundamentalist adherence to the Qur'an and the *hadīth*, the collected accounts and words of the Prophet Muhammad.

One of the most troubling implications in analyses of ISIS's fundamentalism was that non-Muslim people believed the radical group's assertion that they practiced a more authentic version of Islam. Writing for *The Atlantic* in 2015, Graeme Wood argued that denying ISIS's medieval religious nature is "dishonest," and that "much of what the group does looks nonsensical except in light of a sincere, carefully considered commitment to returning civilization to a seventh-century legal environment."[3] Bernard Haykel, a professor of Near Eastern Studies interviewed for Wood's article, declared that ISIS fighters "are smack in the middle of the medieval tradition and are bringing it wholesale into the present day."[4] This is a common misunderstanding about all extremist religions: that being a literal reader of a religious text, and a rigorous adherent to all written religious law, is more "medieval," and therefore more authentic.

Fundamentalist faiths usually claim to practice literal interpretations of the Bible, Qur'an, Torah, or other sacred texts. And while this is certainly as valid a belief system as any other, it isn't actually an *old* way of believing. Literalism is relatively modern. In fact, scholar Karen Armstrong has argued that it coincides with the rise of the scientific method, alongside other literal and statistical approaches to humanities disciplines. American Christian biblical literalism, for instance, didn't begin until the nineteenth century, and it didn't fully take hold in many churches until the end of the twentieth. The Southern Baptist Church's current website declares that the Bible is "God-breathed": "It has God for its author, salvation for its end, and truth, without any mixture of error, for its matter. Therefore all Scripture is totally true and trustworthy."[5] But Southern Baptists themselves did not all agree on the doctrine of biblical inerrancy and literalism until the 1990s, when conservative pastors made it a litmus test for professors at their universities.

Similarly, the Haredim, or "ultra-Orthodox" Jews, who govern their lives by religious texts and shun outside influences, are also a nineteenth-century development, even though they claim to be practicing the oldest and most authentic form of Judaism: "Our differentness only reflects our fealty to the Judaism of the Ages," spokesperson Avri Shafram wrote in *The Forward* in 2014.[6] And Wahhabism, the theology behind what many Americans call "Islamic Fundamentalism," did not emerge until the late eighteenth century. Founded in Saudi Arabia, it died out in other regions until recently, after Saudi charities started funding schools and mosques in the 1970s to promote it across the globe. Although all of these religious movements are considered politically and socially conservative, they are, in fact, *reformist* movements. They set out to change the way their respective faiths have been practiced for centuries in order to make them more restrictive. And they are largely a product of the modern era, not of medieval times.

Medievalism makes extremists believe that their practices have a firm basis in history, and critics of fundamentalist religions use medievalism to accuse religious people of being backwards and ignorant. But both sides are wrong. As you will see, the varieties of religious extremism active today combine all the modes of oppression and violence we've been discussing throughout the book with all the mistaken assumptions about the medieval past, making it a very modern phenomenon.

THE BIBLICAL PATRIARCHY MOVEMENT

IT MAY sound like something out of Margaret Atwood's *Handmaid's Tale*, but the American Biblical Patriarchy movement, once relegated to the radical fringes, is a growing force in the United States.[7] This movement draws on an extreme version of the "complementary genders" theory we described in the previous chapter; it demands female submission and male dominance in marriage and family relations. Young women are considered the property of their fathers until they can marry and bring new Christians into the world. Young men should grow up prepared to be warriors for Christ, and, eventually, the kings of their own household castles.

Biblical Patriarchy proponents believe that their gender enforcement system will both save the Church and solve many of the world's ills. The now-defunct Vision Family Forum's website had a statement on Biblical Patriarchy that claimed,

> The defining crisis of our age is the systematic annihilation of the Biblical family.... Minimize the father and the family will perish.... The sad truth is that broken and weak families are the norm even within the most conservative and doctrinally orthodox church assemblies. This is in large part due to the death of Biblical patriarchy with its emphasis on father-directed vision, leadership, and self-sacrifice.[8]

But although they described their required gender relations as "Biblical," they don't look to late antiquity for their models of behavior. Instead, they use the Middle Ages—or their thin understanding of it—to mold their children into what they think are perfect vessels for Christ.

Biblical Patriarchy proponents often use the language of princesses and kings—a Disney-inspired neomedieval ideal that weirdly omits the prince—to indoctrinate young women into their gender roles. The princess's destiny is to marry a man who will become king and to give birth to future kings.

Female purity, beauty, and desirability to men are at the heart of the princess myth, but so is female passivity, which is required to allow men to be brave, strong, and chivalrous. For instance, Vision Forum Ministries, which was a leading force in the American Evangelical movement before its president, Doug Phillips, was sued for sexual abuse, had a thriving marketplace full of educational products that used medievalism to shape children's gender roles. Supermarket shelves in the American South and Midwest are stocked with this kind of gender-conformist medievalism, such as books like *His Princess: Love Letters from Your King*, which features inspirational letters from God to girls about how to remain modest, feminine, slim, and beautiful.

Nowhere is this medieval symbolism more evident than at the purity ball, a medieval-themed prom at which daughters pledge their virginity to their fathers. Yes, you read that right. Purity balls invite young girls to imagine themselves as medieval princesses and their fathers as powerful "knights" who can protect them from the world. The minor details of each purity ball vary depending on the organization and location. But most contain three ceremonial elements: the "cross dance," in which very young girls—younger than the adolescent daughters who serve as their fathers' dates—parade into the ballroom wearing white tutus and carrying a giant cross; the "covenant," an oath from the father to his daughter inspired by medieval chivalric oaths; and a symbolic ritual sacrifice, in which daughters pass through an archway of crossed swords, then yield their "flowers" to the foot of a giant cross. The whole ritual emphasizes the doctrine that women's sexuality isn't for themselves—it's a commodity protected for and by "kings."

Although there is no official gendered indoctrination ceremony for boys that is equivalent to the purity ball in Evangelical circles, Randy Wilson, the purity ball's founder, recommends a ritual he conducts for his sons called "Brave Heart of a Warrior," in which he gives the boys a purity ring and a sword. Wilson recounts the story of his first son's ceremony on the *Generations of Light Ministry* website: "At that time the immense sword was almost his height. I explained to him that although he could not wage war right now with this imposing sword, he would grow into the weight of the sword just as he would grow into the weight of manhood."[9]

These rituals connect masculinity to violence in the same way they connect a woman's worth to her sexual purity. They bring us back to the unspoken aspects of those complementary gender roles people seem so bent on locating in the Middle Ages: if men are naturally violent, and women must be "pure" to be worthy of male protection, then "impure" women become targets for violence. In other words, it's a recipe for rape culture.

Many people associated with the early Biblical Patriarchy Movement—like Doug Phillips—have lost their leadership positions after being accused of adultery and sexual assault.[10] But its cultural influence has gone mainstream. Vice President Mike Pence embraces purity culture, which sees men as unrestrainable animals and women as vessels of lust, when he refuses to be alone with a woman who is not his wife.[11] Betsy DeVos, Trump's Education Secretary, is known for her radical religious beliefs, and she is imposing purity culture on America's national education system by revising Title IX to make it harder to prosecute rape on campus.[12] And since far-right evangelical Mike Pompeo took over as Trump's Secretary of State, the US has taken pains to block any references to "sexual and reproductive health" in United Nations aid activities.[13]

FAR-RIGHT CATHOLICISM

CHRISTIAN EXTREMIST medievalism isn't limited to Evangelical Protestants. There is also a strand of ultra-conservative Catholicism that embraces medievalism to support a sexist, deeply patriarchal, anti-Jewish, and anti-Muslim worldview. In fact, the SPLC says that radical traditionalist Catholics "may make up the largest single group of serious antisemites in America."[14] These Catholics reject the reforms of the Second Vatican Council, which, as the SPLC writes, "condemned hatred for the Jews and rejected the accusation that Jews are collectively responsible for deicide in the form of the crucifixion of Christ."[15]

Perhaps unsurprisingly, especially since 11 September 2001 and the overall rise in anti-Muslim bigotry around the world, these groups have also added anti-Muslim hatred to their anti-Jewish animus. They often attempt to justify these prejudices—as well as their misogyny—by constructing a heroic image of medieval Catholic knighthood and arguing that the Crusades and even the Inquisition were justified and part of an ongoing "clash of civilizations."

One such group is the American-based organization "Slaves of Immaculate Heart of Mary," who represent themselves as Catholics despite the Vatican demand that they stop doing so in 2017 (and who, likely to the extreme consternation of the Vatican, currently hold the website www.catholicism.org). The extremist view that caught the Vatican's attention was a radical interpretation of the doctrine *extra Ecclesiam nulla salus* ("outside of the Church there is no salvation"). It is easy to see how this doctrine, when taken literally, can fuel anti-Jewish and anti-Muslim bigotry. And that is fully realized by this organization, which publishes frequent articles condemning Muslims and Jews and criticizing the Catholic Church's post-Vatican II attempts to reconcile with other faiths.

Perhaps unsurprisingly, the Slaves of the Immaculate Heart of Mary's propaganda employs a warped interpretation of the Middle Ages as an idyllic, inspirational era. Their website is full of articles with titles like, "Recovering a Bright Medieval Vision for the Future," "Can Chivalry Return?", and "The Thirteenth: The Greatest of Centuries."[16] Clearly, what they like about the Middle Ages is the fantasy of patriarchy, Christian supremacy, and violence against those outside the Church. They are particularly enamored of the Crusades, which they regularly characterize incorrectly as "defensive wars against Islam" that were meant to "reconquer Christian lands."[17] Their website erroneously claims that "much of history since the seventh century has been shaped by an unending conflict between the One True Church and Islam."[18] Of course by now, you, the reader, know better: this is just a particularly fervent example of the fictional "clash of civilizations" narrative we discussed in Chapter Three.

Several other online organizations and influencers churn out content with a radical traditionalist Catholic bent. Perhaps the most successful is "Church Militant" (previously known as "Real Catholic TV," until the Archdiocese of Detroit demanded that they stop using the word *Catholic* in their title in 2012).[19] Church Militant is a multimillion-dollar media organization that produces articles, videos, and podcasts. Alongside rampantly anti-LGBTQ+ content and content attacking "leftists," Muslims, and "globalists" (a common anti-Jewish dog whistle), Church Militant displays an obsession with the medieval past. The site hosts apologetics for the Crusades and the Inquisition. One episode of their online show *The One True Faith*, titled "One True Faith Revisited: The Crusades and the Inquisition," reframes the Crusades as a defensive war by arguing that the Middle East was and should be Christian-held territory and uses the medieval expansion of Islam to argue that the Crusades were justified.

The presenters of the show also argue that the medieval Inquisition (which they distinguish from the Spanish Inquisition) was "a thing of compassion. Christian culture was profused [*sic*] all throughout Europe at the time, and heresy was something that struck at the very root of civilization. [...] it was a way to clear up theological difficulties. It was a great protection to the people of Europe."[20] Finally, they then use this falsely sanitized idea of the medieval Inquisition to spread hatred against Islam by arguing that Muslims are more violent than the medieval Church. Calling the Inquisition an "absolute watchdog for the faith," the hosts argue that at least the Inquisition's punishments weren't "having your nose slit or your hands chopped off," which they insist, incorrectly, were common practices in medieval Muslim countries.[21]

It is easy to see how these revisionist arguments help spread Islamophobia and violence against Muslims, and can even encourage the American invasion of Middle Eastern countries. But these arguments are also historically wrong. The medieval Inquisition *did* use torture. Its punishments included imprisonment for life, forced conversion, and, as demonstrated by the fate of Joan of Arc and hundreds of others, execution. Throughout the Middle Ages, an accusation of heresy was no small matter. But rarely do Christian supremacists acknowledge the truth of medieval history when it inconveniences their anti-Muslim worldview.

Catholic extremists, like their Evangelical counterparts, are also deeply committed to a view of "chivalry" that takes an uncritical, Victorian-vintage view of Christian knighthood. As Charles A. Coulombe wrote for the Slaves of the Immaculate Heart of Mary website in an article titled "Can Chivalry Return?", the organization hopes "to reinject chivalry and—dare it be said—Catholic militancy and masculinity back into the life of the Church."[22] The allegiance between so-called chivalry and patriarchal sexism was on full display in a conference in May 2019 called "Raising Chivalrous Young Men ... in an Increasingly Decadent Society." The website for the conference featured a quote by radio host Mike Church, who organized and headlined the conference, advising participants to take up the mantle of "chivalry" that puts them at the head of their households in order to raise subservient daughters:

> The crisis of a lack of manly formation in our time is real and ruthless in it's [sic] diabolical conquest of so many souls for Hell. This conference is an attempt to put a halt to the slide and begin the process of realigning men, young and old, with their God-given privilege, as professor Dilsaver reminds us, of being the Priest, Prophet and King of their domains. To raise a generation of modest, Christian daughters requires a generation of chivalrous knights to court and defend them; this and nothing less is the lofty goal we must set and aspire to and pray to Our Lady to assist us in.[23]

Perhaps unsurprisingly, considering his own Catholicism, several of these right-wing conservative Catholic men are also fond of the medievalisms of J.R.R. Tolkien. Articles by the Slaves of the Immaculate Heart of Mary regularly discuss Tolkien's work and freely integrate discussions of the fallen Numenoreans (from Tolkien's *Silmarillion*) with their condemnations of Jewish people, who they argue are a fallen "chosen people."[24] They also think the Rohirrim from *The Lord of the Rings* embody chivalric virtues for contemporary men. One speaker at the "Raising Chivalrous Young Men" conference, Joseph Pearce, published two books not just proposing a conservative Catholic interpretation for *The Hobbit* and *The Lord of the Rings* but arguing that this was Tolkien's intent all along.[25]

Though they may have radically different theological beliefs, the similarities between Evangelical and Catholic extremists are striking: both are governed by their attachment to Christian supremacy and male supremacy. And although they see themselves as radically opposed to Islam, they have far more in common with radical Islamic extremists than they do with mainstream Christians. In fact, their apocalyptic rhetoric, their emphasis on violent masculinity and submissive female purity, their obsession with the Crusades, their perpetuation of rape culture, and their desire to force entire nations to follow their religious laws, make them all but indistinguishable from groups like ISIS.

THE MEDIEVAL ISLAMIC "GOLDEN TIME"

LIKE THESE radical Christian groups, ISIS adopted the Crusades rhetoric spread in the wake of 9/11 and used it as a key recruitment strategy. Formed in the wake of the Iraq War, ISIS was not the only radical Islamist group in the Middle East, but it had unprecedented success recruiting soldiers, thanks both to its social media savvy and its deft deployment of medievalism.[26]

ISIS marketed the Middle Ages as a time of lost religious and ideological purity, a "golden time" to which the world should return—under their flag. In ISIS propaganda, the neomedieval caliphate they claimed to have reestablished was just as much a monument to lost power as it was evidence of new power. For ISIS, the medieval Crusades are part of the future as well as the past. For instance, *Dabiq*, an ISIS magazine for Westerners, is named for a town in Syria where ISIS radicals believe they will defeat the "crusaders" and usher in the end of the world.[27] A 2014 issue called *The Failed Crusade* used George W. Bush's own rhetoric to forge links between the Crusades, colonialism, and their new war with America: "The old colonialism was but a front for the crusaders, just as it is today a front for the Jews and Christians. Indeed, the 'Caesar of Rome' Bush has declared multiple times that, 'It is a Crusade!' So why do people lie and deny this?"[28]

ISIS received a lot of attention for its desire to recreate the Crusades, but the tendency of Islamic radicals to appeal to the medieval historicity of their faith predates the rise of ISIS by nearly decade. Journalist Peter "Theo" Curtis, writing as Theo Padnos, delved into the recruitment of young Western Muslims to a radical madrasa in Dammaj in his 2011 book, *Undercover Muslim: A Journey into Yemen*. Curtis (a Muslim convert himself) went undercover at the Dar al-Hadith madrasa, which was known for recruiting young men online, and discovered that they were being sold the fantasy of a renewed medieval "golden time" in a fundamentalist Sunni utopia. The madrasa advocated radical simplicity and "repudiated the 'innovations' (bi'dah) or false traditions which, from century to century, have accrued to the edifice of Islam."[29]

After 9/11 and during the wars in Iraq and Afghanistan, young Muslims found themselves increasingly stereotyped or disenfranchised in North American and European countries. The urge to find a place of acceptance was understandable. But Curtis revealed that this madrasa convinced these young men that they would be able to live like neomedieval caliphs. He describes Westerners who made this journey as particularly privileged in Yemen. Those who acquired Yemeni brides (a man can marry up to four women in Yemen) "were the aristocrats among the students ... to the outside world, wives are a sign of well-being, mastery of the world, prosperity and abundance."[30] Strikingly, Curtis notes that conflict in these marriages often occurred because the husbands, the Western converts, favored a more fundamentalist and more restrictive version of Islam than their Yemeni wives did. They permitted no television in their homes, only allowed strict halal meals, and required girls to wear hijab at six years old instead of the traditional age of nine.[31] The Yemeni Shi'a eventually destroyed the madrasa based on their belief that the Saudi-sponsored university was a shelter for radical Sunni fighters and a front for weapons smuggling. But even though the school is gone, the fantasies that drew its students thrived in ISIS, which declared itself a new caliphate whose mission was to reclaim that lost medieval "golden time."

According to the CIA, at one point there were at least 15,000 foreign fighters in ISIS's ranks, many of whom were Westerners.[32] ISIS recruited young men and women through an online propaganda campaign, including sleek videos that cast young ISIS soldiers as heroes in a glorious epic battle, riding horses and carrying swords. They even used footage from the recent Tolkien film adaptation *The Two Towers*. When ISIS held territory, its medievalism was a mix of actual history and historical fantasy: they revived a medieval tax on non-Muslims in Raqqua, and announced that anyone "deemed an apostate [can] be crucified or beheaded," a law they claimed was medieval.[33] (Historically, however, Muslim scholars disagreed about the death penalty as much as Americans do today.) ISIS also provided bouncy castles with the ISIS logo on them to entertain children. To young men who felt dismissed and disempowered, ISIS recruitment videos and propaganda sold them a life like a neomedieval video game, in which they could star as conquering, fierce warriors. And it sold young women a Disney Middle Ages in which they could be noble princesses, protected and adored by heroic "lions."

Female purity and rape culture were a disturbing part of ISIS's medievalism, just as they are for the religious extremists discussed earlier in this chapter. After all, as you have seen, the use of the Middle Ages to reinforce traditional gender roles is not limited to one religious extremist group, or even to one religion. Under ISIS control, even women who joined the cause willingly had their behavior strenuously controlled: they could not go outside alone, their clothing was rigorously policed, and hospitals were emptied of female doctors. The universities closed, and official ISIS publications stated that "girls [can] be married from the age of nine" and "women should only leave the house in exceptional circumstances and should remain 'hidden and veiled.'"[34]

ISIS perpetrated a horrific campaign of sexual violence against women who did not conform to its narrow standards of purity. They released a 2014 statement in *Dabiq* called "The Revival of Slavery Before the Hour," in which they argued, "One should remember that enslaving the families of the *kuffar*—the infidels—and taking their women as concubines is a firmly established aspect of the Shariah, or Islamic law."[35] Women and girls considered "infidels" reported being stored in a warehouse in Mosul with locked doors and blacked-out windows, forced to take off their head scarves to be assessed for their attractiveness, and, if chosen, dragged out by their hair to be raped.[36] A woman interviewed by *The Guardian* described being held "in a dark hall together with hundreds of other women, and girls. Some of them children who were not more than five years old.... On a daily basis," she explained, "men entered the room to pick out a girl. First the most beautiful girls, the young ones."[37] These reports, along with stories of "adulteresses" being stoned or "witches" being executed by ISIS officials, have fueled some of the accusations that ISIS is "medieval" or "trapped in the Middle Ages."[38] But that makes it all too easy to dismiss just how common violence against women still is in today's world.

ISIS extremists have not been the only ones to embrace the fantasy of a neomedieval crusade in violent rhetoric and propaganda in today's Middle Eastern wars. Christians in America and Europe are also calling for a new crusade—not just the Christians safe at home but also some of the soldiers on the battlefield. Throughout the wars in Iraq and Afghanistan, some extremist Christian soldiers sported Crusades-themed patches meant to inflame their Muslim opponents: images of a medieval knight eating a pig's head that read "PORK-EATING CRUSADER" in both English and Arabic, for instance, or a crusader knight riding a bomber jet, or simply a Crusades cross emblazoned with a skull and the words "Embrace the Hate."[39] The battle against ISIS seemed to give everyone tacit permission to kick their racist Crusades-mongering up a notch, as though both sides want to recreate one of the most pointless stretches of violence in human history. Neither side seems interested in the innocent people trying to live their lives and raise their families in the midst of the warfare and horror these neocrusaders create.

A NEOMEDIEVAL EPIDEMIC

ALTHOUGH MODERN extremists seem obsessed with the Crusades, those wars are not the only medieval inspiration for today's religious violence. Moreover, Christians and Muslims are not the only ones playing medieval games with people's lives. In 2014, for instance, leaders in the Hindu nationalist movement known as *Hindutva* invoked the medieval Muslim and Christian conquests of Hindu cultures as an invasion that needs to be remedied. The leaders of this movement focus most of their anger on local Muslims. One Hindu Nationalist leader, Sanjay Prajapati, claimed in 2014 that Muslims wanted to "convert our daughters to Islam because they feel they can increase their population" and warned that if India did not take action, "we'll soon be their slaves."[40] Champat Rai, another nationalist leader, declared that "Muslims invaded India and used the sword to convert," arguing that because of this, the "motherland" of India should be purely Hindu.[41] Much like the students in Dammaj and the delusional members of the Slaves of the Immaculate Heart of Mary, Hindu Nationalists want to return to their own "golden time," except for them, this means medieval India before the Muslim and Christian invasions. And in 2019, the Indian government used this anti-Muslim fervor to invade Kashmir.

Some pagan movements are also dedicated to resurrecting what they see as lost medieval Norse faiths, which they believe were stolen from them by conquering Christians. The

1960s and 1970s saw a renewed interest in the revival of "pagan" traditions from medieval and pre-medieval European societies and the foundation of a range of faith communities, one of the most popular being Ásatrú (in some places known simply as "Heathenry" or "Heathenism"). Ásatrú has practitioners in about 100 countries and claims over 10,000 adherents. The core tenets of the religion revolve around reviving (or inventing) religious practices tied to the Norse polytheistic traditions. But Ásatrú has also had to contend with a splinter group of its practitioners who are white supremacists and who use the faith as a front for their white nationalist ideology.

Some Ásatrú white supremacists, like Stephen McNallen, have founded entire branches of this faith that promote a white nationalist worldview.[42] Often these groups differentiate themselves from the peaceful, inclusive branches of Ásatrú by calling their faith "Odinism." One member of one such neo-pagan group called the "Wolves of Vinland" burned down a Black American church in 2012. Two other Odinism practitioners were arrested in 2016 over a plot to bomb Black churches and Jewish synagogues in order to start a "race war."[43] Several of the participants in the deadly 2017 "Unite the Right" riot in Charlottesville, Virginia, were identified as prominent members of white nationalist Odinist groups.[44]

Most practitioners of Ásatrú are not part of these white supremacist splinter faiths. It would be wrong to paint an entire religion with the brush of its very worst adherents, just as it would be wrong for us to associate all Christians or all Muslims with extremist neocrusaders. However, thanks in part to the legacy of Nazi Germany, especially its misuses of the medieval past, Odinist groups have a lot of white supremacist history to draw on. Those Ásatrú groups that are not steeped in white supremacy are particularly vigilant about it in their midst.

Ásatrú devotees who are interested in real medieval history have plenty to celebrate, just as contemporary Jews, Muslims, and Christians can look to medieval accomplishments for positive inspiration. As we showed you in earlier chapters, religious and racial intolerance were far from standard practice in the medieval Scandinavian world, where people of different faiths often coexisted peacefully.

BIBLICAL LITERALISM AND MEDIEVAL FAITH

As we mentioned in the introduction to this chapter, there is a widespread misconception that following a stricter interpretation of religious texts hearkens back to medieval times. But that has far more to do with our myths about the Middle Ages than the facts. First of all, most medieval people did not read religious texts literally. In fact, most people could not read them at all because religious texts were not generally written in the vernacular (i.e., in everyday language). The vast majority of medieval Christian texts were written in Latin, which was only read by religious officials, scholars, writers, merchants, and elites. The Qur'an was more often recited in medieval mosques than read, and it was recited in a dialect of classical rather than colloquial Arabic. Classical Arabic, like medieval Latin, was the province of scholars and the elite. Upper-class or scholarly Jewish people wrote in Hebrew, but although Hebrew was a foundation of the languages used by Jewish rabbis and writers for their religious dialogues and scriptural commentaries, it was not a fixed language. Yiddish was the colloquial language of some medieval Jews, while Jews living in Arab lands spoke a dialect known as "Judeo-Arabic," different from Ladino (Judeo-Spanish), and different still from Yiddish.

But even if the language of religious texts had been accessible to the common people, the physical books and scrolls themselves would not be. Books were the province of scholars and clergy, and they were so expensive to produce that they were often chained to desks or locked away to prevent theft. The printing press was not brought to Europe until the end of the Middle Ages; before that, religious texts were all produced by hand. This also meant that there was no singular, authoritative version of many religious texts. Take the Christian Bible, for instance: medieval scribes were notorious for adding their own wording, changing or removing a line, and glossing—adding interpretive advice in the margins of a text. And then there's the issue of translation, that long game of telephone: early versions of texts written in Hebrew, Aramaic, and Greek were translated into later versions of Hebrew and Greek, and those were translated to Latin.

You might also be surprised to learn that in the Middle Ages, Church officials did not even agree on the contents of the Bible. Before the printing press (and in many cases, after), theologians argued about which religious texts were authentic and which weren't. Sacred texts are really compilations of writing: letters, stories, and the testimony of scribes and disciples who recorded what Moses, Jesus, and Mohammad said. In addition to that, many faiths have supplementary texts, like the hadīth in Islam and the Halakha in Judaism, which list laws, miracles, practices, and histories that vary in importance depending on which sect you might belong to or what your local religious leaders prefer.

The Christian Apocrypha are a great example of this. For centuries, early Christians worked with a body of varied and sometimes contradictory texts and debated which ones were "canonical," meaning official or real. The decision-making process was slow—it lasted until the fifth century. The standard medieval bible in Europe was eventually based on Jerome's Latin Vulgate Bible (compiled in 405 CE). It included texts deemed to be non-canonical but did not translate them from Hebrew into Latin. Martin Luther's early Protestant Bible (1534) omitted some Apocrypha and put the rest in its own section. King James Bibles published before 1666 included the Apocrypha, but in 1826, the National Bible Society of Scotland petitioned to have them removed. The "literal" Protestant Bible in its most popular, current form wasn't settled on until the 1800s, and other Christians, like Catholic or Orthodox Christians, still read various parts of the Apocrypha as canonical.

So, even within modern Christianity, there is not one Bible but many. And the story of evolution and revision of the Christian Bible(s) is much the same for other faiths. Hebrew scholars have had centuries of dialogue and debate about the contents of the Torah, the Talmud, and other important texts. In fact, debate and discussion on questions like these are integral to Judaism, especially in the Middle Ages. Muslim scholars have also debated the contents and meaning of the Qur'an and the hadīth throughout the Islamic world, and throughout history.

Because we were well and fully out of the Middle Ages when most laypeople could regularly engage with, argue about, and come up with their own interpretations of religious texts, many medieval people found the spirit of faith far more important than the letter. (This has historically, and disingenuously, been used to argue for the superiority of Christianity over Judaism by people who don't realize just how much thought, intellectual debate, philosophy, logic, and conversation has always been a feature of Jewish faith.) In the medieval world, literal readings were considered simplistic and were strongly advised against. For example, Saint Augustine's *On Christian Doctrine*, written in 426 CE but widely considered authoritative by theologians throughout the Middle Ages, specifically warns against strict literal interpretation. His warning is particularly strong for the reader unskilled in Hebrew and Greek because of how easy it is for translators to make errors: "Many translators are deceived by ambiguity in the original language which they do not understand, so that they transfer the meaning to something completely alien to the writer's intention."[45] Augustine provides several examples, such as how easy it is to confuse plants with baby cows:

> Some, because *móschos* in Greek means "calf," do not know that *moscheúmata* means "transplantings" and have translated it "calves." This error appears in so many texts that one hardly finds anything else written, although the sense is very clear and is supported by the succeeding words. For the expression "bastard slips shall not take deep root" makes better sense than to speak of "calves," which walk on the earth and do not take root in it.[46]

Far from taking everything at surface value, medieval theologians and scholars had sophisticated methods for interpreting the Bible. Dante Alighieri's famous letter to his patron Can Grande Della Scalla describes common medieval interpretive practices that will look familiar to any literature major today (the technical term for these practices is *hermeneutics*). He believed all texts were "polysemous," meaning they have multiple meanings: "for it is one sense which we get through the letter, and another which we get through the thing the letter signifies, and the first is called literal, but the second allegorical or mystic."[47] Allegory, for Dante, is "a truth hidden under beautiful fiction." Dante also believed in two more layers of interpretation: moral, meaning what can be extracted by teachers to enrich themselves and their students, and *anagogic*, "above the senses"—the easiest way to describe this is spiritual reception, a divine connection, or a higher sense of understanding. Reading the "letter"—the surface meaning—of a religious text, for Dante and other medieval scholars, was just the first step on the way to higher spiritual truth, a step that wasn't always trustworthy. This highly complicated way of understanding religious texts is behind the rich allegory of Dante's *Divine Comedy*, which, perhaps ironically, shapes many a modern person's understanding of hell.

Thus, although today's literalist movements claim to be returning to the "roots" of their particular religions, they are actually doing the opposite. They believe the Bible is fully understandable by a layperson with no special training, whereas the roots of their religions are actually filled with educated scholars arguing about mistranslations from the original languages and about hidden layers of meaning.

How people choose to worship within their own faiths is their business. But claims of medieval historicity become a problem when they are used in the service of religious extremism. Because despite the apparent modernity of literalist practice, extremists use the mistaken belief that their literalism is old, authentic, and medieval in order to argue for its superiority. They believe that the whole world should be terraformed to suit their particular way of worshipping. They commit violence within their own communities and against others, and in the worst cases, full-fledged acts of terrorism and war.

VARIETIES OF MEDIEVAL
RELIGIOUS EXPERIENCE

Y OU MIGHT be used to imagining the medieval world as a place where everyone believed the same thing. The Middle Ages in popular culture is an era of superstition, of religious obedience, and of conformity—a world that will brook no dissent or interrogation. But anti-intellectualism was not a feature of medieval religion. In the Middle Ages, the world's three major monotheistic religions—Judaism, Christianity, and Islam—had, at their core, a spirit of interrogation and questioning. (Not to mention that an even larger population of the medieval world was polytheistic.) Medieval religious practice was intellectual and varied. God was supposed to lead you to the truth through a rational, logical process of thought, and every human being was supposed to possess Reason, a gift from God that would lead you back to faith through, not in spite of, using your mind.

That doesn't mean medieval people all believed the same thing, even within their own faiths. For instance, medieval Christianity was more diverse than you might think. Prior to 1054, there were no "Catholic" or "Eastern Orthodox" branches of Christianity, but after years of theological and political disagreements, 1054 CE saw the Great Schism, which split Christianity into those two branches. Then, in the fourteenth century, the Church split again as *two different popes* were elected, one who led from Avignon, France, and the other who led from Rome. European leaders were forced to pick which pope they followed, with each side claiming that the other was led by an "antipope." Things got even more complicated when a third contender for the papacy was elected by another faction, with each claimant excommunicating the other. This led to a religious and diplomatic crisis that lasted for 40 years.

In spite of the fact that many of our sources from the medieval Christian world were written by people involved in the Church, we have as many stories of people rebelling against their strictures as we have of people who adhered to them. The Cathars solved the age-old question of "why does God allow evil to exist in the world" by believing that there were two Gods, one good and one bad. The Pelagians believed that original sin did not exist and that people did not need the Church for morality. And while it was dangerous to be an avowed atheist in medieval Europe, religion wasn't altogether that important for many people. Far from being a universal "Age of Faith," for some laypeople, the demands of religion were an annoying set of social requirements and dietary restrictions rather than a source of fervent belief.

Medieval Christian faith is often imagined by people today as the enemy of progress, but in fact, the opposite was true. Believers embraced science and knowledge; they didn't fear it. Witchcraft trials and the persecution of scientific figures like Galileo are imagined as "medieval," but these events took place after the Middle Ages, during the supposedly intellectually superior Renaissance. In fact, medieval scientists were *part of* the Church, which encouraged research and exploration in fields like medicine, astronomy, philosophy, biology, geography, and logic. Religion and science went hand in hand in Islam and Judaism too: Muslim scholars like al-Battani and al-Zarquali advanced knowledge in astronomy, while others worked in math, science, and geography. Persian scholar al-Khwarizmi even invented algebra. Medieval Jewish scholars like Maimonides wrote that science and philosophy were an integral part of faith, and plenty of Jews served as physicians and pharmacologists.

Nor was the Church the ubiquitous vehicle of gender oppression that people imagine: medieval religious women studied theology, philosophy, science, and medicine. Take Hildegard of Bingen, for example, who wrote two medical books in addition to books on theology, music, and language. In fact, the medieval Church was one of the few vehicles for a medieval woman's education and independence.

And perhaps it's worth noting that despite the emphasis on purity in modern neomedieval extremist movements, medieval people weren't anti-sex.[48] This includes religious people.

Consider the medieval fabliaux, the traditional "dirty story" of the Middle Ages, full of adulterous sex, naked butts, and fart jokes. Wildly popular, and widely read and translated, fabliaux told stories that could curl even our modern toes. French fabliaux had titles like *Le fablel de la crote* ("The Tale of the Turd"), *Les trois dames qui troverent un vit* ("The Three Women Who Found a Dildo"), *De l'annel qui faisoit les vis grans et roides* ("The Ring That Made Dicks Big and Stiff"), and *Du chevalier qui fist les cons parler* ("The Knight Who Made Cunts Speak"). Believe it or not, these fabliaux were mostly written by clergy: they have been found in manuscripts alongside courtly and religious poetry written by the very same author.

Men and women of the cloth were not spared as erotic subjects or object of ridicule in fabliaux either. There was the Old French *Du prestre qui ot mere a force* ("The Priest Who Had a Mother Forced on Him") and *Le Prestre et Alison* ("The Priest and Alison"). Chaucer's infamous *Miller's Tale* involves a clerk, Nicholas, who tricks a religious man into thinking that the biblical flood is coming so he can have sex with the man's wife. *The Shipman's Tale* features a monk who bribes his cousin's wife to have sex with him. In fact, works like Chaucer's *Canterbury Tales* and Boccaccio's *Decameron* brutally and thoroughly parodied most members of the medieval Church—monks, priests, prioresses, and nuns—and put them in graphic and compromising situations. Although some modern religious sensibilities have found these texts offensive (Boston College used to keep its copy of Chaucer locked up in a glass case in the 1950s), medieval people had no such compunctions.

Medieval people could be very frank about sexuality in real life too, and one's sex life was considered an important factor in one's overall health. In medieval England, for instance, if a woman accused her husband of impotence so she could get out of a marriage, a local midwife or sometimes a group of midwives would come over to test whether the allegation was true. (Talk about performance anxiety!) Some medical texts prescribed masturbating a woman to orgasm if she had an excess of cold humors—a particular problem in widows. It's hard to imagine any of today's religious extremists—no matter how much they are accused of being "medieval"—approaching sex with the same frank spirit and clinical distance.

Whenever someone tells you that medieval people were fundamentally different from you—more faithful, more "pure," less individual, or less intelligent—this should raise an immediate red flag. An agenda, and sometimes a violent agenda, lies behind the claim. The truth of history is that there is no simple, unadulterated time to go back to and escape all the diversity and complexity of human life. It wasn't true when the Emperor Augustus longed for it in ancient Rome, and it isn't true now. But that shouldn't make anyone less interested in studying the past. Instead, it should open up whole new worlds to explore and new ways to find connections with other human beings that can stretch across time.

EPILOGUE: THE FUTURE OF THE MEDIEVAL PAST

> You know, films have an ability to show us where we've been, where we are and where we could be. And Wakanda is where we could be....
>
> —Lupita Nyong'o in an interview on her role in *Black Panther*, 2018[1]

THE MIDDLE Ages have been conscripted for a wide range of awful purposes—promoting white supremacy, religious violence, racism, homophobia, and patriarchal oppression. But the past holds promise too. There's a reason so many people have been drawn to the Middle Ages. Some of our most popular heroes—King Arthur, Robin Hood, Saladin, Joan of Arc—come from medieval legend. Your most epic battle today was probably on Twitter or in traffic. But the stakes seem higher when they're set against a medieval landscape: people fighting for their kings, their loves, and their lives. In a world full of drones, emails, and oil changes, many of us quietly envy people who believed that elves lurked in forests, who found power in religious relics, and who lived by the work of their hands. It is easy to get caught up imagining what it might have been like to live in medieval times or to wonder what wisdom the past might hold for our own lives.

In light of all we have written here, it can be tempting to quarantine the Middle Ages, to try to create a society that lives only in the present moment. We have, after all, taken you to some pretty dark places. But we don't intend to leave you there. Medieval history can also enrich your life, help you understand the world around you, and help you imagine a better future.

PLAYING IN THE PAST

Every year, over 10,000 people from around the world gather in a field in rural Pennsylvania. For two weeks each summer, a sleepy rural township is transformed into a carnival of pre-modern pageantry as the members of the Society for Creative Anachronism (SCA) bring their unique brand of history to town. The SCA is one of the world's largest living history groups, and they are devoted to studying and creating their own unique vision of the Middle Ages. But though it is one of the biggest, it is far from the only living history group devoted to medieval times. Each one has a different focus, different rules, and a different vision of the past. The SCA is quite clear about its purpose: many of its members aren't historical reenactors in the strictest sense, married to the idea of authenticity. Instead, as the organization has said in some of its advertising materials, they are creating "the Middle Ages as they should have been, without the strife and pestilence, but with an attempt to preserve the ideals of beauty, grace, chivalry, and fellowship."

The SCA's idealized Middle Ages has not always been free from structural oppression, but plenty of its members look forward while also looking back, creating inclusive spaces to imagine a new Middle Ages. Take for example, Clan Blue Feather—an LGBTQ+ organization within the SCA dedicated to exploring, as they say on their website, "all aspects of sexual or gender associated minority expression in research and education of their place in period as well as advocacy for their concerns and those of our straight allies in the SCA."[2]

It's not just re-enactors who try to imagine, and reimagine, the Middle Ages. Maybe you've participated in a live-action roleplaying game or gone to a medieval festival or renaissance faire. Maybe you're learning swordplay with Historical European Martial Arts (HEMA) groups, or maybe you're a cosplayer with a badass Arya Stark getup that you made by hand. Maybe your medievalism is digital, and you log into your *World of Warcraft* account every day to raid a dungeon for a new set of armor or spend countless hours in *Foundation* crafting a perfect medieval city.

Why do we spend so much time, effort, and money playing in the Middle Ages? None of the medieval worlds we just discussed is the real one (though some make efforts to get closer than others). But that's beside the point. The point, instead, is to be transported to another time, either alone or in a community of peers. Playing in the Middle Ages offers us an escape from the stressors of mundane modern reality, offering an emotionally heightened, romantic backdrop against which we can imagine our lives. Suddenly, we aren't frustrated bank managers or algebra students with 8:00 a.m. exams. We can be rogues, wizards, knights in the queen's service, or even the queen herself.

Approaching the Middle Ages playfully can be one of the most positive ways to transform our relationship to the past and to imagine other possibilities for the future. Game designers have seized on this brand of postmodern medievalism, in which they can pick and choose which elements of the past they want to recreate and which they want to transform, to make more progressive neomedieval spaces that welcome all players. The *Elder Scrolls* and *Dragon Age* franchises, once criticized for racism and sexism, have broadened their digital neomedieval worlds. They still let you fight with swords, ride horses, and drink plenty of ale, but they now feature same-sex partnerships, more racial diversity, transgender characters, and plenty of women warriors. A few hardliners react poorly to these updates and even try to use "history" to back up their claims. But as we hope you've learned from the rest of this book, those "politically correct" insertions usually bring games closer to historical reality—or as close as you can get while you're riding a dragon. Often what we really need to do to touch the past is to rip away the illusions that keep us from seeing the full humanity of medieval people, to see where their experiences were different from our own, and to recognize what we have in common.

MAKING MEDIEVALISM

Mᴇᴅɪᴇᴠᴀʟɪsᴍ ɪsɴ'ᴛ all fun and games. Some participants in the SCA and other reenactment societies work for years to become world-class practitioners of medieval arts and crafts. They join the hundreds of others who have created a cottage industry online of selling handmade objects—hand-bound books, handmade furniture, home-brewed beer and mead, and even handmade swords and armor—either through their own small businesses or on websites like Etsy and eBay. The question is: why? Why take the time and effort to create things by hand (and spend the considerable money to buy them), when factories can churn out the same objects at a fraction of the cost?

Each craftsperson likely has a unique answer. But as we can learn from medievalism's revival in the nineteenth century, the labor is part of the point. William Morris, a nineteenth-century publisher, translator, designer, author, and artist, was a leader in the Victorian "Arts and Crafts" movement, which valued both handmade objects and the process of making them. Morris sought to restore the glories of medieval crafts-manship in the face of what he felt were the dehumanizing, destructive effects of the Industrial Revolution.[3] For Morris, a return to the Middle Ages meant turning away from the exploitative natures of capitalism and towards craftsmanship and individual artistry. He took inspiration from the Middle Ages, especially from medieval craft guilds, and promoted the idea that learning and practicing these medieval crafts was a virtue in and of itself. He was also a political activist, even founding socialist organizations throughout his life.

Likewise, A.W.N. Pugin, one of the most famous architects of the nineteenth-century Gothic Revival, which used medieval architecture as its inspiration, designed a number of medieval-style buildings, including the Palace of Westminster and the tower that holds Big Ben. He also wrote several landmark books on architecture in which he explained why he was so passionate about recreating medieval designs. He ended one of his books, *Contrasts: Or a Parallel between the Noble Edifices of the Middle Ages, and Corresponding Buildings of the Present day; Shewing the Present Decay of Taste*, with this statement of purpose:

> I wish to pluck from the [current] age the mask of superior attainments so falsely assumed, and I am anxious to direct the attention of all back to the real merit of past and better days. It is among their remains that excellence is only to be found; and it is by studying the zeal, talents, and feelings, of these wonderful but despised times, that art can be restored, or excellence gained.[4]

In other words, Pugin's project was not just about buildings but about society. He didn't just want to rehabilitate the image of the Middle Ages from the (literal and figurative) ruination that had befallen it. He wanted to bring his own society back to a more medieval world.

If Morris and Pugin sound like they could be part of the twenty-first century "Maker Movement," that's because their ideology was very similar and because they were inspired by the same disenchantment with a technological world. In the twenty-first century, the information revolution and the globalization of labor have devalued human work, placed an unprecedented amount of wealth in the hands of a few, and created a world in which everything is disposable.

Makers and other neomedieval artisans are launching a quiet rebellion against industrial and technological excesses. They value maintaining a link to the past, repairing rather than throwing away, and prioritizing the personal over the mass-manufactured. For example, Linette Withers is a professional bookbinder who has her own business and works on repairing books in the oldest library in Leeds, England. When asked in a 2019 personal interview why she binds books, she said:

> The object I finish with is not only beautiful to me but also very practical. They are objects that I know someone will use and even if only in a very mundane sense fill with bits

of themself. Sometimes possibly deeply important bits of themself.

And by repairing books, I'm keeping not only the book's content going, but also (depending on how my customer feels, admittedly) its context. I am working with what the previous binder has done, and maintaining that link to the past. Part of me is quite excited by the idea that some future binder may work to conserve a book I've bound.[5]

Medieval martial arts practitioners in HEMA and the SCA have similar motivation. Reviving medieval martial practices is intensely demanding, and to many of us, it also seems pretty daunting. None of us will have to fight for our lives with a sword in a duel or on the battlefield. In fact, there are plenty of reasons *not* to practice HEMA, including the ever-present risk of bodily harm! But enthusiasts do it to learn about a fascinating subject, to better themselves, to feel a connection to the past, and to keep a once-lost tradition alive. Swedish HEMA fencer Anders Linnard explains why he participates in HEMA in a 2015 documentary about the sport entitled *Back to the Source: Historical European Martial Arts*: "By doing this, it connects us to the past. It creates a context that is a bit anachronistic in the modern world, but that's also the appeal of it. We want to do this because it's part of a heritage and a tradition that people are missing in the modern world where everything changes all the time."[6] In other words, the medieval martial arts practice is grounding. Adopting practices, crafts, and ways of engaging with the world from a time when streetlights didn't drown out all the stars and your phone wasn't constantly sending you notifications, can help people find focus, peace, and even learn more about themselves.

None of these movements is immune to the pitfalls of nostalgic extremism that we see in other attachments to the medieval past. Each one has to guard its borders—from the "makers" who bring Nazi-themed jewelry to craft fairs or the medieval martial arts practitioners who sexually harass women or commit acts of racist violence. But in this sense, technology has been a boon, allowing neomedieval groups to expose the violence and hatred in their groups and excise it by sharing information and reinforcing rules that keep their "medieval" spaces tolerant and safe.

FANTASY MEDIEVALISMS

MEDIEVAL-THEMED FANTASY literature has had an enormous influence on the movements we've described in this chapter—often far more so than actual literature from the Middle Ages. But fantasy's relationship to the Middle Ages has been a troubled one. Even one of the foundational authors of modern fantasy, J.R.R. Tolkien, reflects sexism and racism in his books. As scholar Helen Young has argued, Tolkien created different groups of people with distinct abilities and characteristics (elves, dwarves, men, hobbits) and gave them the label "race."[7] In his *Lord of the Rings* trilogy, the white "Men of the West" are pitted against Sauron's evil forces, who ally with people of color from the east and south.

Tolkien's biases may have been a product of his time, but his conservative medievalism has been further enhanced by his imitators and derivatives in the decades since. Influential medieval fantasy roleplaying games like Dungeons and Dragons added mathematics to Tolkien's racial divisions, meaning there is now a racialized "bell curve" of ability scores for each of the playable fantasy races. Some of the most famous additions that D&D writers have added to the fantasy canon, such as the evil, dark elves known as the "Drow," are also rooted in the deeply racist idea that non-white people are inherently bad.

Thankfully, some authors, filmmakers, and game designers are working today to make a fantasy medievalism more inclusive. The progress over the last ten years is especially promising as audiences have opened up to more diverse, and more accurate, ideas of what constitutes "medieval." Just ten years ago, many games didn't even offer playable female characters, and playable people of color were few and far between. In *Dragon Age: Origins*, playing as a woman meant fielding constant interrogation and criticism in-game about why a woman was fighting.[8] The game was set in Ferelden, an alternate version of England, and featured almost no POC characters. By the time the third *Dragon Age* title was released in 2014, it featured POC companions and non-player characters, transgender heroes, multiple same-sex romances, and a gender-neutral world (including realistic armor for female avatars instead of the dreaded "boobplate"). Despite the complaints of a few angry racist and sexist gamers who organized online, the third *Dragon Age* was Bioware's best-selling game to date.[9]

A new generation of writers, game designers, filmmakers, and TV writers is constantly imagining broader engagements with the medieval world. Recent fantasy novels like Saladin Ahmed's *Throne of the Crescent Moon* and S.A. Chakraborty's Daevabad Trilogy guide readers through landscapes inspired by *1001 Nights* and the medieval Middle East. *Kingdom*, a new show set in medieval Korea, is a smash hit on Netflix. In 2015, Indian director Gunasekhar released the epic film *Rudhramadevi*, based on a thirteenth-century medieval ruler who disguised herself as a man to rule as a monarch. Evan Winter's *Rage of Dragons* combines traditional fantasy tropes with African influences, R.F. Kuang's *The Poppy War* is set in a fantasy version of China, and Naomi Novik's *Spinning Silver* reimagines a medieval fairy-tale world with a Jewish main character. Thanks to all of these brilliant creators, no fantasy fan has to be stuck in a sexist, homophobic, all-white medieval Europe anymore.

Some of the most promising medievalisms come from the playful mix of medieval and modern, or even combining fantasy medievalism with futurism and science fiction. Two of the most successful Marvel franchise films to date have been prime examples of this: *Black Panther* and *Thor: Ragnarok*. *Black Panther* is, on its surface, an Afrofuturist story about a superhero who comes from an uncolonized part of Africa.

But as scholar Matthew Vernon argues, *Black Panther* also blends Afrofuturism and medievalism freely.[10] Wakanda's warriors wield swords and shields along with high-tech spears, wear neomedieval armor, and drape themselves in furs.

While the film takes its costumes, props, design, and language from a wide range of cultures across the African continent, several commentators have drawn specific historical parallels between the Kingdom of Wakanda and medieval Ethiopia.[11] Ethiopia was the only African country to successfully rebuff European colonization, and, in the Middle Ages, it was a powerful mountainous kingdom with trading and diplomatic connections across the region. Medievalism is also woven into *Black Panther*'s plot: a lost prince's return, a king's exile, and a grand battle between right and wrong for the crown would not be out of place in a medieval romance. In short, *Black Panther* is a story that successfully draws upon the past but with an eye firmly looking toward the future.

Thor: Ragnarok also draws on the Middle Ages for its source material and mixes it with futuristic tech. Like all films in the *Thor* franchise, *Ragnarok* features figures and scenes drawn from the *Prose Edda* and the *Poetic Edda*, which are our main source material for Norse theology. The franchise has always been more diverse than many racist viewers would like: the casting of Idris Elba as Norse god Heimdall in the first film caused significant backlash online. But *Ragnarok*, directed by Taika Waititi, integrates anti-racist narratives into its medievalism and puts the evils of colonialism front and center.[12] *Ragnarok* is not just a tale from history—it's about how history is altered and misused, showing how Europeans brutally conquered Indigenous peoples and then recast themselves as saviors and benevolent gods. In one particularly telling scene, the antagonist Hela details how the Asgardians whitewashed their blood-soaked history of conquest with the image of themselves as deities. The film dramatically illustrates this in a scene where the celebratory ceiling frescoes in Asgard's throne room are torn away to reveal the much darker images of death and oppression beneath. Since you've read this book, you know how white supremacists appropriate medieval Norse culture and use it for violent ends. Well, *Thor: Ragnarok* knows it too, and it purposely strips away that narrative to strike at the heart of historicized racism.

Not every piece of creative medievalism is as revolutionary and progressive as *Black Panther* and *Thor: Ragnarok*. But they don't all have to be. The success of both these films shows us how hungry audiences are for positive, progressive, forward-looking medievalisms rather than medievalism rooted in outmoded, toxic ideas.

HOPE FOR THE FUTURE

T HE MIDDLE Ages has just as much to offer those who want to make the world more inclusive, more forward-looking, and a more humane place as it does to those who would do otherwise. And the medieval past has plenty of inspiration for progressive projects: powerful women who fight their own battles; men who spin their love for other men into beautiful poetry; and thriving cultural centers where Christians, Muslims, and Jews share ideas about philosophy, science, and faith. We can tell stories out of Africa, Persia, and China as well as Europe. We can find people committed to the cause of peace and harmony, and heroic figures for a vast diversity of people to look up to. And most of all, we can have a laugh at the things that bind us all together, like fart jokes and bad sex.

The stories we choose to tell about the past can define how we see the present, and change what we want the future to be. People have been misusing the Middle Ages for a long time. But there is plenty of room, and plenty of medieval material, to tell a new set of stories about the past. And through these stories, we can create a more vibrant, compassionate, and connected future.

NOTES

Introduction: Weaponizing History

1. Livy, *The Early History of Rome*, trans. Aubrey de Sélincourt (London: Penguin, 2002), 30.
2. Elizabeth Carson Pastan and Stephen D. White with Kate Gilbert, *The Bayeaux Tapestry and Its Contents: A Reassessment* (Woodbridge, UK: The Boydell Press, 2014).
3. David W. Blight, *Race and Reunion: The Civil War in American Memory* (Cambridge, MA: The Belknap Press, 2001); James W. Loewen and Edward H. Sebesta, eds., *The Confederate and Neo-Confederate Reader: The "Great Truth" about the "Lost Cause"* (Jackson: University Press of Mississippi, 2018).
4. Mitch Landrieu, "Mitch Landrieu's Speech on the Removal of Confederate Monuments in New Orleans," *New York Times*, 23 May 2017, https://www.nytimes.com/2017/05/23/opinion/mitch-landrieus-speech-transcript.html.
5. Amy S. Kaufman, "In the Shadows of Rome: Building an Arthurian England," *Groniek* 43, no. 189 (March 2010): 383–97, 384–85.
6. For just a few examples: Rabia Umar Ali, "Medieval Europe: The Myth of Dark Ages and the Impact of Islam," *Islamic Studies* 51, no. 2 (Summer 2012): 155–68; David Matthews, *Medievalism: A Critical History* (Woodbridge, UK: D.S. Brewer, 2015); Robert Houghton, "Reigns: The Great, Simple, King Simulator with a 'Dark Ages' Problem," *The Public Medievalist*, 3 October 2019, https://www.publicmedievalist.com/reigns/.

1 The Middle Ages: Foundational Myths

1. Umberto Eco, *Travels in Hyperreality*, trans. William Weaver (San Diego: Harcourt, 1986), 65.
2. For example, between 1611 and 1618, almost 400 individuals were killed in witch hunts in the city of Ellwangen; witch hunting was particularly bad in the southern and western regions of what is now Germany. See Brian P. Levack, *The*

Witch-Hunt in Early Modern Europe, 3rd ed. (London: Routledge, 2013).

3. Leonardo Bruni, *History of the Florentine People: Volume I, Books I–IV*, ed. James Hankins (Cambridge, MA: Harvard University Press, 2001), xvii–xviii.

4. Johannes Fried, *The Middle Ages*, trans. Peter Lewis (Cambridge, MA: The Belknap Press, 2015), vii–viii.

5. Giovanni Andea Bussi, *Prefazioni alle edizioni di Sweynheym e Pannartz prototipografi romani*, ed. M. Miglio (Milan: Ed. "il Polifilio," 1978), 7; Angelo Mazzocco, ed., *Interpretations of Renaissance Humanism* (Leiden: Brill, 2006), 112.

6. Eco, *Travels in Hyperreality*, 68.

7. Chaucer adapted several tales from Boccaccio's *Decameron* in his *Canterbury Tales*. Shakespeare used Boccaccio as source material for *All's Well That Ends Well*, *Cymbeline*, and *The Two Gentlemen of Verona*. Tennyson adapted Boccaccio for his 1879 poem "The Lover's Tale," and Keats adapted him in his 1818 poem "Isabella, or the Pot of Basil." Pasolini directed a 1971 film called *The Decameron*, and Baena adapted a Boccaccio tale for his 2017 film *The Little Hours*.

8. Paul B. Sturtevant, "What Politicians Mean When They Call the Border Wall 'Medieval,'" *The Washington Post*, 22 January 2019, https://www.washingtonpost.com/outlook/2019/01/22/what-politicians-mean-when-they-call-border-wall-medieval/.

9. See, for instance, "'Medieval Murder': 19 Illegal Immigrant MS-13 Members Charged with 'Savage' Killings across LA," *Sean Hannity*, 17 July 2019, https://hannity.com/media-room/medieval-murder-19-illegal-immigrant-ms-13-members-charged-with-savage-killings-across-la/; and "Siege of Syria's Eastern Ghouta 'Barbaric and Medieval,' Says UN Commission of Inquiry," *UN News*, 20 June 2018, https://news.un.org/en/story/2018/06/1012632. For medievalism rhetoric during America's wars in Iraq and Afghanistan, see Bruce Holsinger, *Neomedievalism, Neoconservatism, and the War on Terror* (Chicago: Prickly Paradigm Press, 2007).

10. Marianne O'Doherty, "Where Were the Middle Ages?" *The Public Medievalist*, 7 March 2017, https://www.publicmedievalist.com/where-middle-ages/; Geraldine Heng, "Afterword: Medievalists and the Education of Desire," in *Whose Middle Ages: Teachable Moments for an Ill-Used Past*, eds. Andrew Abin, Mary C. Erier, Thomas O'Donnell, Nicholas L. Paul, and Nina Rowe (New York: Fordham University Press, 2019); Bryan C. Keene, ed., *Toward a*

Global Middle Ages: Encountering the World Through Illuminated Manuscripts (Los Angeles: The J. Paul Getty Museum, 2019).

11. See, for instance, William Manchester Little, *A World Lit Only by Fire: The Medieval Mind and the Renaissance, Portrait of an Age* (Boston: Little, Brown, 1992); and Stephen Greenblatt, *The Swerve: How the World Became Modern* (New York: W.W. Norton, 2011).

12. On 27 January 2020, Virginia became the thirty-eighth state to ratify the ERA. However, it is currently unclear what this means for the amendment, as several other states are bringing lawsuits arguing that the deadline for ratification has passed. Time, and the courts, will tell what the outcome will be. Veronica Stracqualursi, "Virginia reaches long-awaited milestone by ratifying Equal Rights Amendment, but legal fight looms," *CNN.com*, 27 January 2019, https://www.cnn.com/2020/01/27/politics/virginia-equal-rights-amendment-trnd/index.html.

13. Monica H. Green, *The* Trotula: *An English Translation of the Medieval Compendium of Women's Medicine* (Philadelphia: University of Pennsylvania Press, 2002).

14. Monica H. Green, *Making Women's Medicine Masculine: The Rise of Male Authority in Pre-Modern Gynaecology* (Oxford: Oxford University Press, 2008).

15. Adam Simmons, "Uncovering the African Presence in Medieval Europe," *The Public Medievalist*, 27 April 2017, https://www.publicmedievalist.com/uncovering-african/; Helen Young, "Where Do the 'White Middle Ages' Come From?" *The Public Medievalist*, 21 March 2017, https://www.publicmedievalist.com/white-middle-ages-come/.

2 Nationalism and Nostalgia

1. Jeremy Diamond and Kevin Liptak, "Trump Calls Border Wall a 'Medieval Solution' that Works," *CNN.com*, 9 January 2019, https://www.cnn.com/2019/01/09/politics/trump-executive-authority-border/index.html.

2. Benedict Anderson, *Imagined Communities: Reflections on the Origin and Spread of Nationalism* (London: Verso, 1991).

3. Andrew B.R. Elliott, *Medievalism, Politics and Mass Media: Appropriating the Middle Ages in the Twenty-First Century* (Woodbridge, UK: D.S. Brewer, 2018); Vladimir Soldatkin,

"Putin Unveils Monument to Russia's 'Spiritual Founder,'" Calls for Unity," *Reuters*, 4 November 2016, https://www .reuters.com/article/us-russia-monument/putin-unveils -monument-to-russias-spiritual-founder-calls-for-unity -idUSKBN12Z1MV; John Lichfield, "The 600-Year Struggle for the Soul of Joan of Arc," *The Independent*, 5 January 2012, https://www.independent.co.uk/news/world/europe/the -600-year-struggle-for-the-soul-of-joan-of-arc-6284992.html.

4. José Ortega y Gasset, *España Invertebrada*, trans. Mildred Adams (New York: Howard Fertig, 1974), 20–22.

5. Louis L. Snyder, *Roots of German Nationalism* (Bloomington: Indiana University Press, 1978), 39.

6. Jacob Grimm and Wilhelm Grimm, *The Complete Grimm's Fairy Tales*, trans. Margaret Hunt and James Stern (New York: Pantheon Books, 1944), 943.

7. *The Saga of the Volsungs*, trans. Jesse L. Byock (London: Penguin Books, 1999), 72.

8. The following discussion of King Arthur is an adaptation of Amy S. Kaufman, "In the Shadows of Rome: Building an Arthurian England," *Groniek* 43, no. 189 (March 2010): 383–97.

9. Alfred, Lord Tennyson, *Tennyson: A Selected Edition*, ed. Christopher Ricks (Abingdon, UK: Routledge, 2007), 679.

10. Thomas R. Metcalf, *The New Cambridge History of India, III.4: Ideologies of the Raj* (Cambridge: Cambridge University Press, 1995), 72–76.

11. This section is an expansion, revision, and adaptation of Paul B. Sturtevant, "Mel Gibson, You Magnificent Bastard," *The Public Medievalist*, 31 July 2015, https://www .publicmedievalist.com/braveheart-independence/.

12. Colin McArthur, *Brigadoon, Braveheart and the Scots: Distortions of Scotland in Hollywood Cinema* (London: I.B. Tauris, 2003), 126.

13. Richard Hayton, "The UK Independence Party and the Politics of Englishness," *Political Studies Review* 14, no. 3 (2016): 400–10, https://doi.org/10.1177/1478929916649612.

14. The tweet was removed after the candidate came under criticism for it. ITV Report, "UKIP Candidate Apologises for Retweeting Offensive Image of St George Lancing the Prophet Mohammed," *ITV News*, 27 April 2015, https://www.itv .com/news/london/2015-04-27/ukip-candidate-apologises-for -retweeting-offensive-image-of-st-george-lancing-the-prophet -mohammed/.

15. William Booth, Tom Hamburger, Rosalind S. Helderman, and Manuel Roig-Franzia, "How the 'Bad Boys of Brexit' Forged Ties with Russia and the Trump Campaign—and Came Under Investigators' Scrutiny," *The Washington Post*, 28 June 2018, https://www.washingtonpost.com/politics/how-the-bad-boys -of-brexit-forged-ties-with-russia-and-the-trump-campaign --and-came-under-investigators-scrutiny/2018/06/28/6e3a5e9c -7656-11e8-b4b7-308400242c2e_story.html.
16. This section is an adaptation and expansion of Amy S. Kaufman, "Muscular Medievalism," *The Year's Work in Medievalism* 31 (2016): 56–66 and Paul B. Sturtevant, "What Politicians Mean When They Call the Border Wall 'Medieval,'" *The Washington Post*, 29 January 2019, https://www.washingtonpost.com/outlook/2019/01/22 /what-politicians-mean-when-they-call-border-wall-medieval/.
17. Chris Cillizza, "Donald Trump Used a Word He's 'Not Supposed To.' Here's Why," *CNN*, 23 October 2018, https:// www.cnn.com/2018/10/23/politics/donald-trump-nationalism /index.html.
18. Remarks by Donald J. Trump, Campaign Speech in Clairesville, Ohio, June 2016, https://www.youtube.com /watch?v=RhQU6lnU77Q.
19. Al Weaver, "Chuck Schumer: Border Wall Is 'A Medieval Solution for a Modern Problem,'" *The Washington Examiner*, 9 December 2019, https://www.washingtonexaminer.com/chuck -schumer-border-wall-is-a-medieval-solution-for-a-modern -problem; Dick Durbin (@SenatorDurbin), "As of today, the President's pursuit of a medieval wall has forced hundreds of thousands of federal workers to miss a payday. He's holding their paychecks hostage to fulfill a shortsighted campaign promise. It is cruel," Twitter, 11 January 2019, https://twitter .com/SenatorDurbin/status/1083783437767634945; Hakeem Jeffries (@RepJeffries), "We are not paying a $5 billion ransom note for your medieval 🏰 border wall. And nothing you just said will change that cold, hard reality. Not happening. Get. Over. It," Twitter, 8 January 2019, https://twitter.com/RepJeffries /status/1082822559920517120.
20. "Remarks by President Trump in Roundtable on Border Security | McAllen, TX," *The White House*, 10 January 2019, https://www.whitehouse.gov/briefings-statements/remarks -president-trump-roundtable-border-security-mcallen-tx/.
21. Reagan used the "shining city" metaphor repeatedly throughout his political career but employed it most famously

in his election eve "A Vision for America" address in 1980 and his farewell address in 1989. Ronald Reagan, "Election Eve Address, 'A Vision for America,'" *The American Presidency Project*, 3 November 1980, https://www.presidency .ucsb.edu/documents/election-eve-address-vision-for-america; Ronald Reagan, "Farewell Address to the Nation," *The American Presidency Project*, 11 January 1989, https://www .presidency.ucsb.edu/documents/farewell-address-the-nation.

22. Salvador Rizzo, "A Caravan of Phony Claims by the Trump Administration," *The Washington Post*, 25 October 2018, https://www.washingtonpost.com/politics/2018/10/25 /caravan-phony-claims-trump-administration/.

23. Caitlin O'Kane, "18-Year-Old U.S. Citizen Detained by Border Officials Said Conditions Were So Bad He Lost 26 Pounds, Almost Self-Deported," *CBS News*, 26 July 2019, https:// www.cbsnews.com/news/us-citizen-detained-by-ice-francisco -erwin-galicia-border-officials-conditions-bad-almost-self -deported/.

24. Hannah Rappleye and Lisa Riordan Seville, "24 Immigrants Have Died in ICE Custody during the Trump Administration," *NBC News*, 9 June 2019, https://www .nbcnews.com/politics/immigration/24-immigrants-have-died -ice-custody-during-trump-administration-n1015291.

25. Dina Khapeva, "Putin's Medieval Dreams," *Project Syndicate*, 29 December 2017, https://www.project-syndicate.org /commentary/russia-resurrecting-ivan-the-terrible-eurasianism -by-dina-khapaeva-2017-12.

26. Jonathan Marcus, "Putin: Russian President Says Liberalism 'Obsolete,'" *BBC News*, 28 June 2019, https://www.bbc.com /news/world-europe-48795764.

27. Agence France-Presse in Ankara, "Abbas Welcomed at Turkish Presidential Palace by Erdoğan—and 16 Warriors," *The Guardian*, 12 January 2015, https://www.theguardian.com/world/2015/jan/12/ abbas-erdogan-16-warriors-turkish-presidential-palace.

28. Paulo Pachá, "Why the Brazilian Far Right Loves the European Middle Ages," *The Pacific Standard*, 18 February 2019, https://psmag.com/ideas/why-the-brazilian-far-right -is-obsessed-with-the-crusades.

29. Geraldine Heng, "The Global Middle Ages: An Experiment in Collaborative Humanities, or Imagining the World, 500–1500 C.E.," *English Language Notes* 47, no. 1, (2009): 205–16. For the numerous research publications of the Global Middle Ages

project, see http://globalmiddleages.org/research-and-teaching;
for a complicating viewpoint, see Robert I. Moore, "A Global
Middle Ages?" in *The Prospect of Global History*, eds. James
Belich, John Darwin, Margaret Frenz, and Chris Wickham
(Oxford: Oxford University Press, 2016), 80–92.

30. Chapurukha Kusimba and Paul B. Sturtevant, "Recovering a
'Lost' Medieval Africa: Interview with Chapurukha Kusimba,
Part I," *The Public Medievalist*, 30 March 2017, https://www
.publicmedievalist.com/recovering-medieval-africa/.

31. For a reasonably accessible introduction to this view of the
Mongol Empire, see Jack Weatherford, *Genghis Khan and the
Making of the Modern World* (New York: Crown Publishers,
2004).

32. Stephanie L. Hathaway and David W. Kim, *Intercultural
Transmission in the Medieval Mediterranean* (London:
Continuum, 2012); James P. Helfers, ed., *Multicultural Europe
and Cultural Exchange in the Middle Ages and Renaissance*
(Turnhout: Brepols, 2005).

33. Matteo Salvadore, *The African Prester John and the Birth of
Ethiopian-European Relations, 1402–1555* (Abingdon, UK:
Routledge, 2017).

34. Andrew Wawn, *The Vikings and the Victorians: Inventing the
Old North in Nineteenth-century Britain* (Woodbridge, UK:
D.S. Brewer, 2000).

35. For a readable introduction to Viking history, see Julian D.
Richards, *The Vikings: A Very Short Introduction* (Oxford:
Oxford University Press, 2005).

36. Usha Vishnuvajjala, "The Strange Medievalism of Mitt
Romney," *Medieval Electronic Multimedia* (blog), 27 April
2013, http://medievalelectronicmultimedia.org/blog/?p=32.

37. Patricia Southern, *Roman Britain: A New History, 55 BC–AD
450* (Stroud, UK: Amberley Publishing, 2012).

3 The "Clash of Civilizations"

1. María Rosa Menocal, *The Ornament of the World: How
Muslims, Jews, and Christians Created a Culture of Tolerance
in Medieval Spain* (New York: Little, Brown, 2002), 11.

2. Jonathan Montpetit, "Whites Risk Marginalization, Mosque
Shooting Suspect Told Friend a Day before Attack," *CBC*, 3
February 2017, https://www.cbc.ca/news/canada/montreal
/alexandre-bissonnette-trump-travel-ban-quebec-mosque
-shooting-1.3966687.

3. Nicole Chavez, Emanuella Grinberg, and Eliott C. McLaughlin, "Pittsburgh Synagogue Gunman Said He Wanted All Jews to Die, Criminal Complaint Says," *CNN.com*, 31 October 2018, https://www.cnn.com/2018/10/28/us/pittsburgh-synagogue -shooting/index.html.

4. Philip Bump, "The Trump Show: Recent Violence Reflects Trump's Rhetoric, Even If It Isn't Powered by It," *The Washington Post*, 28 October 2018, https://www.washingtonpost .com/politics/2018/10/28/trump-show-recent-violence-reflects -trumps-rhetoric-even-if-it-isnt-powered-by-it/.

5. Daniel Wollenberg, "The New Knighthood: Terrorism and the Medieval," *postmedieval* 5, no. 1 (2013): 22.

6. Brenton Tarrant, "The Great Replacement," unpublished manifesto.

7. Imran Awan, "The Non-Muslims Experiencing Islamophobic Attacks," *The New Statesman*, 18 October 2017, https:// www.newstatesman.com/politics/staggers/2017/10/non -muslims-experiencing-islamophobic-attacks; Sarah Parvini, "Being Sikh in Trump's America," *Los Angeles Times*, 11 June 2017, https://www.latimes.com/local/california /la-me-trump-sikhs-20170509-htmlstory.html; Torsten Ove, "Bethel Park Man Gets Probation, Community Service in Federal Hate Crime Assault," *Pittsburgh Post-Gazette*, 6 April 2018, https://www.post-gazette.com/local/south /2018/04/06/Bethel-Park-Jeffrey-Burgess-probation-community -service-federal-hate-crime-assault/stories/201804060128.

8. Deborah E. Lipstadt, *Antisemitism Here and Now* (New York: Schocken Books, 2019); Khaled A. Beydoun, *American Islamophobia: Understanding the Roots and Rise of Fear* (Oakland: University of California Press, 2018).

9. This section on Nazi Germany is an adaptation and expansion of Amy S. Kaufman, "Purity," *Medievalism: Key Critical Terms*, eds. Elizabeth Emery and Richard Utz (Cambridge: D.S. Brewer, 2014), 199–206.

10. Adolf Hitler, *Mein Kampf*, trans. Ralph Manheim (Boston: Houghton Mifflin, 1943), 325.

11. Laurie A. Finke and Martin B. Shichtman, *King Arthur and the Myth of History* (Gainesville: University Press of Florida, 2004). See also Finke and Shichtman, *Cinematic Illuminations: The Middle Ages on Film* (Baltimore: Johns Hopkins University Press, 2010), and Finke and Shichtman, "Exegetical History: Nazis at the Round Table," *postmedieval* 5, no. 3 (2014), 278–94.

12. The archaeologist in question was Franz Altheim; his easily debunked "research" did not prevent him from receiving professorships at the University of Halle and the Free University of Berlin after the war. Heather Pringle, *The Master Plan: Himmler's Scholars and the Holocaust* (New York: Hachette Books, 2006).

13. Christa Kamenetsky, *Children's Literature in Hitler's Germany: The Cultural Policy of National Socialism* (Athens: Ohio University Press, 1984).

14. Eitan Bar-Yosef, "The Last Crusade? British Propaganda and the Palestine Campaign, 1917–18," *Journal of Contemporary History* 31, no. 1 (January 2001): 87.

15. Vivian Gilbert, *The Romance of the Last Crusade: With Allenby to Jerusalem* (New York: D. Appleton and Company, 1923), 171.

16. Mike Horswell, *The Rise and Fall of British Crusader Medievalism, c. 1825–1945* (Abingdon, UK: Routledge, 2018); Ralph E.C. Adams, *The Modern Crusaders* (London: Routledge and Sons, 1920); Cyril A. Alington, *The Last Crusade* (London: Oxford University Press, 1940); John N. More, *With Allenby's Crusaders* (London: Heath Cranton, 1923).

17. Nasar Meer, "Islamophobia and Postcolonialism: Continuity, Orientalism and Muslim Consciousness," *Patterns of Prejudice* 48, no. 5 (October 2014): 500–15, https://doi.org/10.1080/0031322X.2014.966960.

18. Paul B. Sturtevant, "SaladiNasser: Nasser's Political Crusade in El Naser Salah Ad-Din," in *Hollywood in the Holy Land*, eds. Nickolas Haydock and Ed Risden (Jefferson, NC: McFarland, 2009), 123–46.

19. Jonathan Phillips, *The Life and Legend of the Sultan Saladin* (New Haven, CT: Yale University Press, 2019).

20. Phillips, *The Life and Legend of the Sultan Saladin*.

21. Samuel P. Huntington, "The Clash of Civilizations?" *Foreign Affairs* 72, no. 3 (Summer 1993): 22–49, https://doi.org/10.2307/20045621; Samuel P. Huntington, *The Clash of Civilizations and the Remaking of World Order* (New York: Simon & Schuster, 1996).

22. Huntington, "The Clash of Civilizations," 22.

23. "Remarks by the President upon Arrival: The South Lawn," *The White House: President George W. Bush*, 16 September 2001, https://georgewbush-whitehouse.archives.gov/news/releases/2001/09/20010916-2.html.

24. Osama bin Laden, "The Ladenese Epistle: Declaration of War," 23 August 1996, https://scholarship.tricolib.brynmawr .edu/bitstream/handle/10066/4784/OBL19960823.pdf.

25. Osama bin Laden, "World Islamic Front Statement Urging Jihad against Jews and Crusaders," in *Al Qaeda in its Own Words,* eds. Gilles Kepel and Jean-Pierre Milelli, trans. Pascale Ghazaleh (Cambridge, MA: The Belknap Press of Harvard University Press, 2008), 53–56.

26. James Pinkerton, "Century In, Century Out—It's Crusade Time," *Newsday*, 4 December 2003, https://web.archive.org /web/20131024145450/http://newamerica.net/node/6322.

27. Niall Fergusson, *Civilization: The West and the Rest* (New York: Penguin, 2011); *Civilization: Is the West History?* directed by Adrian Pennink, presented by Niall Fergusson, aired Channel 4 (UK), 6 episodes (March–April 2011).

28. This section is an adaptation of Amy S. Kaufman, "To Russia, with Love: Courting a New Crusade," *The Public Medievalist*, 18 February 2017, https://www.publicmedievalist.com /russia-love/.

29. Peter Beinart, "Why Trump's Party Is Embracing Russia," *The Atlantic*, 12 December 2016, https://www.theatlantic.com /politics/archive/2016/12/the-conservative-split-on-russia/510317/.

30. Feder, J. Lester, "This Is How Steve Bannon Sees the Entire World," *Buzzfeed News*, 15 November 2016, https://www .buzzfeednews.com/article/lesterfeder/this-is-how-steve -bannon-sees-the-entire-world#.qiELBV6Bp.

31. *Torchbearer*, directed by Stephen K. Bannon, hosted by Phil Robertson, ARC Entertainment, 7 October 2016, https://www.amazon.com/Torchbearer-Phil-Robertson/dp /B01LZEAEXC.

32. Elizabeth Chuck, Ali Velti, and Andrew Blankenstein, "Trump Campaign CEO Steve Bannon Accused of Anti-Semitic Remarks by Ex-Wife," *NBC News*, 27 August 2016, https://www.nbcnews.com/politics/2016-election/trump -campaign-ceo-steve-bannon-accused-anti-semitic-remarks -ex-n638731.

33. Amy S. Kaufman, "To Russia, with Love."

34. Diana Butler Bass, "For Many Evangelicals, Jerusalem Is about Prophecy, not Politics," *CNN*, 14 May 2018, https:// www.cnn.com/2017/12/08/opinions/jerusalem-israel -evangelicals-end-times-butler-bass-opinion/index.html.

35. Christian Caryl, "How Vladimir Putin Became the World's Favorite Dictator," *The Washington Post*, 8 May 2018, https://

www.washingtonpost.com/news/democracy-post/wp/2018/05/08
/how-vladimir-putin-became-the-worlds-favorite-dictator.

36. Miranda Blue, "Fischer Praises Putin, Calls Him A 'Lion
of Christianity,'" *Right Wing Watch*, 10 October 2013,
https://www.rightwingwatch.org/post/fischer-praises-putin
-calls-him-a-lion-of-christianity; Patrick J. Buchanan, "Putin's
Paleoconservative Moment," *The American Conservative*,
17 December 2013, https://www.theamericanconservative.com
/putins-paleoconservative-moment/.

37. Malcolm Nance, "MSNBC Terrorism Analyst Malcolm Nance
on Russia, Election 2016, and His Perceptions of Donald
Trump's Appointees So Far," interview by Joy Reid, *AM Joy*,
MSNBC, 19 November 2016, https://www.facebook.com
/amjoyshow/videos/1232430470161977/.

38. The next two sections have been adapted and expanded
from Amy S. Kaufman, "A Tale of Two Europes: Jews in the
Medieval World," *The Public Medievalist*, 20 June 2017,
https://www.publicmedievalist.com/tale-two-europes-jews
-medieval-world.

39. Eileen Sullivan, "Trump Again Accuses American Jews of
Disloyalty," *The New York Times*, 21 August 2019, https://
www.nytimes.com/2019/08/21/us/politics/trump-jews
-disloyalty.html.

40. *The Book of John Mandeville*, ed. Tamarah Kohanski and C.
David Benson (Kalamazoo, MI: Medieval Institute Publications,
2007), 83. Translations for this book by Amy S. Kaufman.

41. Geoffrey Chaucer, *The Riverside Chaucer*, ed. Larry D.
Benson, 3rd edition (Boston: Houghton Mifflin, 1987), 211.
Translations for this book by Amy S. Kaufman.

42. Michael Costen, *The Cathars and the Albigensian Crusade*
(Manchester: Manchester University Press, 1997), 123.

43. Eliezar bar Nathan, "Persecutions of 1066," in *The Siege
of Jerusalem*, ed. and trans. Adrienne Williams Boyarin
(Peterborough, ON: Broadview Press, 2014), 142.

44. Albert of Aachen, "History of the Journey to Jerusalem," in
Boyarin, *Siege of Jerusalem*, 139.

45. William of Newburgh, "William of Newburgh's Account," in
The Jews in Christian Europe: A Source Book, 315–1791, eds.
Jacob R. Marcus and Marc Saperstein (Pittsburgh: Hebrew
Union College Press, 2015), 103–4.

46. Geraldine Heng, *Empire of Magic: Medieval Romance and the
Politics of Cultural Fantasy* (New York: Columbia University
Press, 2004), 17–62.

47. Raymond d'Aguilers, "The Conquest of Jerusalem from the *Historia Francorum*," in *Muslim and Christian Contact in the Middle Ages: A Reader*, ed. Jarbel Rodriguez (Toronto: University of Toronto Press, 2015), 63.
48. Raymond d'Aguilers, "The Conquest of Jerusalem," 65.
49. Amin Maalouf, *The Crusades through Arab Eyes*, trans. Jon Rothschild (New York: Schocken Books, 1984), 50–51.
50. Maalouf, *Crusades through Arab Eyes*, 39.
51. Ibn Sārah, "Pool with Turtles," *Poems of Arab Andalusia*, trans. Cola Franzen (San Francisco: City Lights Books, 1989), 40.
52. Robert Chazan, "The Arc of Jewish Life in the Middle Ages," *The Public Medievalist*, 26 September 2017, https://www.publicmedievalist.com/arc-of-jewish-life/.
53. María Rosa Menocal, *The Arabic Role in Medieval Literary History* (Philadelphia: University of Pennsylvania Press, 1983).
54. Henry Chu, "Welcome Back, 500 Years Later: Spain Offers Citizenship to Sephardic Jews," *Los Angeles Times*, 1 October 2015, https://www.latimes.com/world/europe/la-fg-spain-sephardic-jews-20151001-story.html.
55. *The Book of John Mandeville*, 56.

4 White (Supremacist) Knights

1. William Wells Brown, "Narrative of the Life and Escape of William Wells Brown," in *William Wells Brown: A Reader*, ed. Ezra Greenspan (Athens: University of Georgia Press, 2008), 63.
2. The following three sections have been adapted from Amy S. Kaufman, "Anxious Medievalism: An American Romance," *The Year's Work in Medievalism* 22 (2008): 5–13; Kaufman, "Purity," *Medievalism: Key Critical Terms* (2014), 199–206; Kaufman, "A Brief History of a Terrible Idea: The 'Dark Enlightenment,'" *The Public Medievalist*, 9 February 2017, https://www.publicmedievalist.com/dark-enlightenment; and Kaufman, "The Birth of a National Disgrace: Medievalism and the KKK," *The Public Medievalist*, 21 November 2017, https://www.publicmedievalist.com/birth-national-disgrace.
3. Mark Twain, *Life on the Mississippi* (New York: Harper & Brothers Publishers, 1883), 328.
4. Thomas Dixon, *The Clansman: A Historical Romance of the Ku Klux Klan* (New York: A. Wessels Company, 1907), 319.

5. Dixon, *The Clansman*, 326.
6. Dixon, *The Clansman*, 316.
7. "Ku Klux Klan Issues 'Warning,'" *The Daily Progress*, 19 July 1921, https://search.lib.virginia.edu/catalog/uva-lib:2119725/view#openLayer/uva-lib:2119726/4046/3967/2/1/1.
8. Liam Stack, "Leader of a Ku Klux Klan Group Is Found Dead in Missouri," *The New York Times*, 13 February 2017, https://www.nytimes.com/2017/02/13/us/kkk-leader-death-frank-ancona.html.
9. Howard Goodloe Sutton, "Time for the Ku Klux Klan to Night Ride Again," *Democrat-Reporter*, 14 February 2019.
10. Lisa Wade, "How 'Benevolent Sexism' Drove Dylann Roof's Racist Massacre," *The Washington Post*, 21 June 2015, https://www.washingtonpost.com/posteverything/wp/2015/06/21/how-benevolent-sexism-drove-dylann-roofs-racist-massacre/.
11. "KKK Flyers Distributed in Chilliwack Worry Residents," *CBC News*, 28 July 2016, https://www.cbc.ca/news/canada/british-columbia/chilliwack-kkk-flyers-1.3699955.
12. Kaufman, "The Birth of a National Disgrace."
13. Yair Rosenberg, "'Jews Will Not Replace Us': Why White Supremacists Go After Jews," *The Washington Post*, 14 August 2017, https://www.washingtonpost.com/news/acts-of-faith/wp/2017/08/14/jews-will-not-replace-us-why-white-supremacists-go-after-jews/.
14. Paul B. Sturtevant, "Leaving 'Medieval' Charlottesville," *The Public Medievalist*, 17 August 2017, https://www.publicmedievalist.com/leaving-medieval-charlottesville/; Washington Post Staff, "Deconstructing the Symbols and Slogans Spotted in Charlottesville," *The Washington Post*, 18 August 2017, https://www.washingtonpost.com/graphics/2017/local/charlottesville-videos/.
15. Hewes Spencer and Richard Pérez-Peña, "Murder Charge Increases in Charlottesville Protest Death," *The New York Times*, 14 December 2017, https://www.nytimes.com/2017/12/14/us/charlottesville-fields-white-supremists.html; Daniel Victor, "Third Man Arrested in Beating of Black Man at Charlottesville Rally," *The New York Times*, 11 October 2017, https://www.nytimes.com/2017/10/11/us/charlottesville-beating-arrest.html.
16. Walter Henry Cook, "Secret Political Societies in the South during the Period of Reconstruction: Part II," *The Southern Magazine* 3, no. 2 (August–September 1936): 14–17, http://www.confederateneoconfederatereader.com/detail

/the-nadir-of-race-relations/the-united-daughters-of-the
-confederacy-defends-the-ku-klux/.

17. Brad Schrade, "Georgia Women's College Quietly Drops
    Names Tied to Klan History," *The Atlanta Journal-
    Constitution*, 6 August 2018, https://www.ajc.com/news
    /georgia-women-college-quietly-drops-class-names-tied
    -klan-history/sHK31DimvmFhCUTceEvTPP/.

18. Seyward Darby, "The Rise of the Valkyries: In the Alt-Right,
    Women Are the Future, and the Problem," *Harper's Magazine*,
    September 2017, https://harpers.org/archive/2017/09/the
    -rise-of-the-valkyries.

19. Alexandra Minna Stern, *Proud Boys and the White
    Ethnostate: How the Alt-Right Is Warping the American
    Imagination* (Boston: Beacon Press, 2019).

20. Morton W. Bloomfield, "Reflections of a Medievalist:
    America, Medievalism, and the Middle Ages," *Medievalism
    in American Culture: Papers of the 18th Annual Conference
    of the Center for Medieval and Early Renaissance Studies*
    (Binghamton, NY: SUNY Center for Medieval and
    Renaissance Texts and Studies, 1989), 13–27; Eugene D.
    Genovese, "The Southern Slaveholders' View of the Middle
    Ages," *Medievalism in American Culture: Papers of the
    18th Annual Conference of the Center for Medieval and
    Early Renaissance Studies* (Binghamton, NY: SUNY Center
    for Medieval and Renaissance Texts and Studies, 1989),
    31–52.

21. For a full list of books by the scholars mentioned here, please
    see the Further Reading section.

22. Paul B. Sturtevant and Amy S. Kaufman, eds., "TPM Special
    Series: Race, Racism and the Middle Ages," *The Public
    Medievalist*, 2017, https://www.publicmedievalist.com
    /race-racism-middle-ages-toc/.

23. A few examples include Matthew Gabriele, "The Medievalist
    Who Fought Nazis with History," *Forbes*, 23 October 2019,
    https://www.forbes.com/sites/matthewgabriele/2018/10/23
    /medievalist-who-fought-nazis/; David M. Perry, "How to
    Fight 8chan Medievalism—and Why We Must," *The
    Pacific Standard*, 27 June 2019, https://psmag.com/ideas
    /how-to-fight-8chan-medievalism-and-why-we-must-notre
    -dame-christchurch; and Dorothy Kim, "White Supremacists
    Have Weaponized an Imaginary Viking Past: It's Time to
    Reclaim the Real History," *Time*, 15 April 2019, https://time
    .com/5569399/viking-history-white-nationalists/.

24. *People of Color in European Art History*, last modified March 2019, https://medievalpoc.tumblr.com/.

25. See devilshistorians.com.

26. Sierra Lomuto and Adam Miyasharo write regularly for *In the (Medieval) Middle*, http://www.inthemedievalmiddle.com and *Medievalists of Color*, https://medievalistsofcolor.com; see also Mary Rambaran-Olm, "Anglo-Saxon Studies, Academia, and White Supremacy," *Medium*, 27 June 2018, https://medium .com/@mrambaranolm/anglo-saxon-studies-academia-and -white-supremacy-17c87b360bf3.

27. Eli Saslow, "The White Flight of Derek Black," *The Washington Post*, 15 October 2016, https://www.washingtonpost.com /national/the-white-flight-of-derek-black/2016/10/15.

28. Krista Tippett, "Derek Black and Matthew Stevenson: How Friendship and Quiet Conversations Transformed a White Nationalist," *On Being*, 17 May 2018, https://onbeing .org/programs/how-friendship-and-quiet-conversations -transformed-a-white-nationalist-may2018/.

29. Christine de Pizan, *The Book of the City of Ladies*, trans. Earl Jeffrey Richards (New York: Persea Books, 1982), 52.

30. For two recent studies, see Geraldine Heng, *The Invention of Race in the European Middle Ages* (Cambridge: Cambridge University Press, 2018); and Cord J. Whitaker, *Black Metaphors: How Modern Racism Emerged from Medieval Race-Thinking* (Philadelphia: University of Pennsylvania Press, 2019).

31. Sir Thomas Malory, *Le Morte d'Arthur*, vol. 1, ed. P.J.C. Field (Cambridge: D.S. Brewer, 2013), 223. Translations for this book by Amy S. Kaufman.

32. Suzanne Conklin Akbari, "From Due East to True North: Orientalism and Orientation," in *The Postcolonial Middle Ages*, ed. Jeffrey Jerome Cohen (New York: Palgrave, 2000), 23–24.

33. Chrétien de Troyes, *The Complete Romances of Chrétien de Troyes*, trans. David Staines (Bloomington: Indiana University Press, 1990), 16, 97.

34. Ibn Sa'īd al-Maghribī, "Black Horse with White Chest," in *Poems of Arab Andalusia*, trans. Cola Franzen (San Francisco: City Lights Books, 1989), 69.

5 Knights in Shining Armor and Damsels in Distress

1. Judith M. Bennett, *History Matters: Patriarchy and the Challenge of Feminism* (Philadelphia: University of Pennsylvania Press, 2006), 83.

2. Rachael Brown, "George R.R. Martin on Sex, Fantasy, and *A Dance with Dragons*," *The Atlantic*, 11 July 2011, https://www.theatlantic.com/entertainment/archive/2011/07 /george-rr-martin-on-sex-fantasy-and-a-dance-with -dragons/241738/.

3. This section has been adapted from Amy S. Kaufman, "Chivalry Isn't Dead: But It Should Be," *The Washington Post*, 7 October 2018, https://www.washingtonpost.com /outlook/2018/10/08/chivalry-isnt-dead-it-should-be/.

4. Susan Griffin, "Rape: The All-American Crime," *Ramparts* 10 (1971): 30.

5. Chrétien de Troyes, *Complete Romances*, 186.

6. Malory, *Le Morte d'Arthur*, 97.

7. Samuel N. Rosenberg and Carleton W. Carroll, trans., *Lancelot-Grail: Lancelot, Parts I and II* (Cambridge: D.S. Brewer, 2010), 113.

8. Chaucer, *Riverside Chaucer*, 120.

9. See, for example, Yunte Huang, "Read This and Blush: Naughty Medieval French Tales," *The Daily Beast*, 11 July 2017, https://www.thedailybeast.com /read-this-and-blush-naughty-medieval-french-tales.

10. Sir Walter Scott, *Ivanhoe: A Romance* (New York: Penguin Books, 2000), 249.

11. Material in this section has been adapted from Amy S. Kaufman, "Anxious Medievalism," 5–13; "His Princess: An Arthurian Family Drama," *Arthuriana* 22, no. 3 (2012), 41–56; and "Purity," *Medievalism: Key Critical Terms*, 199–206.

12. Brett McKay, "Respecting Our Differences," *The New York Times*, 31 July 2013, http://www.nytimes.com/roomfordebate /2013/07/30/can-chivalry-be-brought-back-to-life/chivalry-is -a-nod-to-differences-between-the-sexes.

13. Richard J. Evans, *The Third Reich in Power* (New York: Penguin, 2006), 332.

14. Evans, *The Third Reich in Power*, 331.

15. Andrew Aglin, "Departure of a Comrade," *The Daily Stormer*, 30 March 2015.

16. John Eldredge, *Wild at Heart: Discovering the Secrets of a Man's Soul* (Nashville: Thomas Nelson, 2001), 16.

17. Eldredge, *Wild at Heart*, 22.

18. Eldredge, *Wild at Heart*, 15.

19. This section has been adapted from Kaufman, "Muscular Medievalism," 56–66. See also Shiloh Carroll, *Medievalism* in *A Song of Ice and Fire and* Game of Thrones (Cambridge: D.S. Brewer, 2018).

20. "Walk of Punishment," *Game of Thrones* season 3, episode 3, written and directed by David Benioff and D.B. Weiss, HBO, aired 14 April 2013.
21. Jace Lacob, "'*Game of Thrones*' Sexual Politics," *The Daily Beast*, 5 June 2011, http://www.thedailybeast.com /articles/2011/06/05/game-of-thrones-sexual-politics.html.
22. National Criminal Justice Reference Center, "Victims of Sexual Violence," *RAINN*, https://www.rainn.org/statistics /victims-sexual-violence.
23. Katty Kay, "Military Rape: Saxby Chambliss, Hormones, and Problems at the Top," *BBC News*, 4 June 2013, https://www .bbc.com/news/world-us-canada-22760944.
24. Colby Itkowitz, Beth Reinhard, and David Weigel, "Trump Compares Himself to Kavanaugh in Latest Sexual Assault Allegation," *The Washington Post*, 22 June 2019, https:// www.washingtonpost.com/politics/trump-compares-himself -to-kavanaugh-in-latest-sexual-assault-allegation/2019 /06/22/81e2c1b4-9509-11e9-aadb-74e6b2b46f6a_story.html.
25. Will Storr, "The Rape of Men," *The Guardian*, 17 July 2011, https://www.theguardian.com/society/2011/jul/17 /the-rape-of-men.
26. Nathaniel Penn, "'Son, Men Don't Get Raped,'" *GQ*, 2 September 2014, https://www.gq.com/story/male-rape-in-the-military.
27. Malory, *Le Morte d'Arthur*, 194.
28. Malory, *Le Morte d'Arthur*, 633.
29. Malory, *Le Morte d'Arthur*, 510.
30. William Rosen, *The Third Horseman: Climate Change and the Great Famine of the 14th Century* (New York: Penguin, 2014), 7.
31. *Gawain on Marriage: The De Coniuge Non Ducenda*, trans. A.G. Rigg (Toronto: Pontifical Institute of Medieval Studies, 1986).
32. Marie de France, *The Lais of Marie de France*, trans. Robert Hanning and Joan Ferrante (Grand Rapids, MI: Baker Books, 2000), 112–13.
33. Jacqueline Murray, "Twice Marginal and Twice Invisible: Lesbians in the Middle Ages," in *Handbook of Medieval Sexuality*, eds. Vern L. Bullough and James A. Brundage (New York: Garland Publishing, 1996), 191–222.
34. Sahar Amer, *Crossing Borders: Love between Women in Medieval French and Arabic Literatures* (Philadelphia: University of Pennsylvania Press, 2013), 17–18.
35. For our purposes, we will retain the gendered pronouns used by the author, but you could just as validly use male or gender-neutral pronouns when discussing Silence.

36. Heldris of Cornwall, *Silence*, trans. Sarah Roche-Mahdi (East Lansing: Michigan State University Press, 1999), 119.
37. Heldris, *Silence*, 123.
38. Heldris, *Silence*, 125.

6 Medievalism and Religious Extremism

1. Edward Gibbon, *The History of the Decline and Fall of the Roman Empire, Complete*, 12 vols., ed. David Widger (Project Gutenberg, 2008), 1:102, https://www.gutenberg.org /files/25717/25717-h/25717-h.htm#Alink2HCH0001.
2. Brad Allenby, "The Return to Medievalism," *Slate*, 18 March 2015, https://slate.com/technology/2015/03/isis-and -other-neomedievalists-reject-technology-modernity.html; Adrian Lee, "The New Dark Ages: The Chilling Medieval Society ISIS Extremists Seek to Impose in Iraq," *The Daily Express*, 21 June 2014, https://www.express.co.uk/news /world/483920/Iraq-Isis-Extremists-Dark-Ages-Muslim -Baghdad-Jihadist; Anoosh Chakelian, "Nick Clegg: 'It's Not Obvious' What the UK Can Do Legally on New Terror Powers in ISIL," *New Statesman*, 2 September 2014, https:// www.newstatesman.com/politics/2014/09/nick-clegg-it-s-not -obvious-what-uk-can-do-legally-new-terror-powers.
3. Graeme Wood, "What ISIS Really Wants," *The Atlantic*, March 2015, https://www.theatlantic.com/magazine /archive/2015/03/what-isis-really-wants/384980/.
4. Wood, "What ISIS Really Wants."
5. "Resolution on Biblical Scholarship and the Doctrine of Inerrancy," *Southern Baptist Convention*, 2012, http://www .sbc.net/resolutions/1225/on-biblical-scholarship-and-the -doctrine-of-inerrancy.
6. Ezra Glinter, "Orthodoxy's Inconvenient Truths," *The Forward*, 13 July 2014, https://forward.com/culture/311651 /orthodoxys-inconvenient-truths/.
7. Material in this section has been adapted from Amy S. Kaufman, "His Princess," 41–56.
8. "The Tenets of Biblical Patriarchy," *Vision Forum Ministries*, https://web.archive.org/web/20130427004848/http://www .visionforumministries.org/home/about/Biblical_patriarchy .aspx.
9. Randy Wilson, "What about Boys," *Generations of Light Ministry*, 2008, http://www.generationsoflight.com/html /boys.html.

10. Amanda Marcotte, "Woman Sues Christian Right Leader Douglas Phillips for Alleged Sexual, Mental Abuse," *Slate*, 16 April 2014, https://slate.com/human-interest/2014/04/douglas-phillips-lawsuit-woman-alleges-sexual-mental-abuse-against-the-former-president-of-vision-forum.html.

11. Aaron Blake, "Mike Pence Doesn't Dine Alone with Other Women. And We're All Shocked," *The Washington Post*, 30 March 2017, https://www.washingtonpost.com/news/the-fix/wp/2017/03/30/mike-pence-doesnt-dine-alone-with-other-women-and-were-all-shocked/.

12. Andrew Kreighbaum, "College Groups Blast DeVos Title IX Proposal," *Inside Higher Ed*, 31 January 2019, https://www.insidehighered.com/news/2019/01/31/higher-ed-groups-call-major-changes-devos-title-ix-rule.

13. Colum Lynch, "Trump Administration Steps Up War on Reproductive Rights," *Foreign Policy*, 18 September 2019, https://foreignpolicy.com/2019/09/18/trump-administration-steps-up-war-on-reproductive-rights/.

14. "Radical Traditional Catholicism," *SPLC Extremist Files*, https://www.splcenter.org/fighting-hate/extremist-files/ideology/radical-traditional-catholicism.

15. "Radical Traditional Catholicism."

16. Brother André Marie, "Recovering a Bright Medieval Vision for the Future," *Catholicism.org*, 1 May 2019, https://catholicism.org/ad-rem-no-341.html; Charles A. Coulombe, "Can Chivalry Return?" *Catholicism.org*, 3 September 2012, https://catholicism.org/can-chivalry-return.html; Sister Marie Pierre, "The Thirteenth: The Greatest of Centuries," *Catholicism.org*, 5 November 2009, https://catholicism.org/the-thirteenth-the-greatest-of-centuries.html.

17. Brother André Marie, "The Crusades: Just Wars?" *Catholicism.org*, 3 February 2016, https://catholicism.org/ad-rem-no-263.html.

18. Gary Potter, "Islam Versus the Faith," *Catholicism.org*, 2 February 2008.

19. Michael Sean Winters, "Real Catholic TV? Not So Much," *National Catholic Reporter*, 27 December 2011, https://www.ncronline.org/blogs/distinctly-catholic/real-catholic-tv-not-so-much.

20. Church Militant, "One True Faith Revisited: The Crusades and the Inquisition," *ChurchMilitant.com*, 26 May 2017, https://www.churchmilitant.com/news/article/otf-the-crusades-and-the-inquisition.

21. Church Militant, "One True Faith Revisited."

22. Charles A. Coulombe, "Can Chivalry Return?"

23. Mike Judge, "Raising Chivalrous Young Men ... in an Increasingly Decadent Society," *The Crusade Channel*, https://www.mikechurch.com/shop/raising-chivalrous-young-men-in-an-increasingly-decadent-society/.

24. Charles A. Coulombe, "Tolkien and Reality," *Catholicism .org*, 5 July 2019, https://catholicism.org/tolkien-and-reality .html.

25. Joseph Pearce, *Bilbo's Journey: Discovering the Hidden Meaning of* The Hobbit (Charlotte, NC: Saint Benedict Press, 2012); Joseph Pearce, *Frodo's Journey: Discovering the Hidden Meaning of* The Lord of the Rings (Charlotte, NC: Saint Benedict Press, 2015).

26. This section has been adapted from Amy S. Kaufman, "Dark Revivals: Medievalism and ISIS," *The Public Medievalist*, 16 October 2014, https://www.publicmedievalist.com /dark-revivals-medievalism-isis, and Kaufman, "Muscular Medievalism," 56–66.

27. William McCants, *The ISIS Apocalypse: The History, Strategy, and Doomsday Vision of the Islamic State* (New York: Macmillan, 2015).

28. ISIS, "The Failed Crusade," *Dabiq* 4, 11 October 2014.

29. Theo Padnos, *Undercover Muslim: A Journey into Yemen* (London: The Bodley Head, 2011), 7.

30. Padnos, *Undercover Muslim*, 112–13.

31. Padnos, *Undercover Muslim*, 117.

32. James Harkin, "How the Islamic State Was Won: Interviews with Fighters, Enemies, and Potential Recruits," *Harper's Magazine*, November 2014, https://harpers.org/archive/2014/11 /how-the-islamic-state-was-won/.

33. Harkin, "How the Islamic State Was Won."

34. Mona Mahmood, "Double-Layered Veils and Despair ... Women Describe Life under ISIS," *The Guardian*, 17 February 2015, https://www.theguardian.com/world/2015/feb/17/isis-orders -women-iraq-syria-veils-gloves.

35. ISIS, "The Failed Crusade," *Dabiq*.

36. "Sexual Violence under ISIS Control," *On Point*, National Public Radio, 25 September 2014 and Rukmini Callimachi, "ISIS Enshrines a Theology of Rape," *New York Times*, 13 August 2015, https://www.nytimes.com/2015/08/14 /world/middleeast/isis-enshrines-a-theology-of-rape.html.

37. Annabell Van den Berghe, "Humiliation Replaces Fear for the Women Kidnapped by ISIS," *The Guardian*, 19 October 2014, http://www.theguardian.com/world/2014/oct/19/isis-forced-marriage-syria-iraq-women-kidnapped.
38. Kareem Shaheen, "Isis Militants Behead Two Syrian Women for Witchcraft," *The Guardian*, 30 June 2015, https://www.theguardian.com/world/2015/jun/30/isis-militants-behead-syrian-women-witchcraft.
39. Anonymous source, personal interview with Amy S. Kaufman, Murfreesboro, TN, April 2015.
40. Julie McCarthy, "In India, Hindu Nationalists Feel Their Moment Has Arrived," *NPR.org*, 26 August 2014, https://www.npr.org/sections/parallels/2014/08/26/343177139/in-india-hindu-nationalists-feel-their-moment-has-arrived.
41. McCarthy, "In India."
42. Sarah Lyons, "Racists Are Threatening to Take Over Paganism," *Vice.com*, 2 April 2018, https://www.vice.com/en_us/article/59kq93/racists-are-threatening-to-take-over-paganism.
43. "Principals in Race War Plot Said to Practice Neo-Pagan Asatru Religion," *SPLC Intelligence Report*, 17 February 2016, https://www.splcenter.org/fighting-hate/intelligence-report/2016/principals-race-war-plot-said-practice-neo-pagan-asatru-religion.
44. Sigal Samuel, "What to Do When Racists Try to Hijack Your Religion," *The Atlantic*, 2 November 2017, https://www.theatlantic.com/international/archive/2017/11/asatru-heathenry-racism/543864/.
45. Saint Augustine, *On Christian Doctrine*, trans. D.W. Robertson, Jr. (New York: Macmillan, 1958), 45.
46. Saint Augustine, *On Christian Doctrine*, 45.
47. Dante Alighieri, *Letter to Can Grande, The Latin Works of Dante* (London: Temple Classics, 1904) 346–52, http://sites.fas.harvard.edu/~chaucer/special/authors/dante/cangrand.html.
48. Information on fabliaux in this section has been adapted from Amy S. Kaufman, "Fabliaux," *Encyclopedia of Medieval British Literature*, eds. Sian Echard and Robert Rouse (West Sussex: John Wiley & Sons, 2017).

Epilogue: The Future of Medieval Past

1. Joe Deckelmeier, "Lupita Nyong'o Interview: Black Panther," *Screenrant*, 8 February 2018, https://screenrant.com/black-panther-lupita-nyongo-interview/.

2. "Clan Blue Feather," *Bluefeather.org*, http://www.bluefeather.org/.

3. Marcus Waithe, *William Morris's Utopia of Strangers: Victorian Medievalism and the Ideal of Hospitality* (Cambridge: D.S. Brewer, 2006).

4. A.W.N. Pugin, *Contrasts: Or a Parallel between the Noble Edifices of the Middle Ages, and Corresponding Buildings of the Present Day; Shewing the Present Decay of Taste* (London: A.W.N. Pugin, 1836), 35.

5. Linette Withers (Consultant Bookbinder, The Leeds Library), personal interview with Paul B. Sturtevant, March 2019.

6. Cédric Hauteville, dir., *Back to the Source: Historical European Martial Arts*, 2015, https://www.youtube.com/watch?v=7DBmNVHTmNs.

7. David M. Perry, "How Can We Untangle White Supremacy from Medieval Studies?: A Conversation with Australian Scholar Helen Young," *The Pacific Standard*, 9 October 2017, https://psmag.com/education/untangling-white-supremacy-from-medieval-studies. For more on this from Dr. Young, see our recommended reading list.

8. Bioware, *Dragon Age: Origins*, Electronic Arts, PC, 2009.

9. Mark Darrah (@BioMarkDarrah), "On to Dragon Age: Inquisition where we switched to Frostbite. Bioware's most highly decorated and selling game (so far)," Twitter, 20 April 2018, https://twitter.com/biomarkdarrah/status/987517890403299328?lang=en.

10. Matthew Vernon, "Whose Middle Ages? Remembering Early African-American Efforts to Claim the Past," *The Public Medievalist*, 23 October 2018, https://www.publicmedievalist.com/whose-middle-ages/.

11. Blue Telusma, "Ethiopians Say Wakanda Not a Far Cry from Reality," *The Grio*, 27 February 2018, https://thegrio.com/2018/02/27/ethiopians-wakanda-black-panther/; Paul Schemm, "Africa's Real Wakanda and the Struggle to Stay Uncolonized," *The Washington Post*, 27 February 2018, https://www.washingtonpost.com/news/worldviews/wp/2018/02/27/africas-real-wakanda-and-the-struggle-to-stay-uncolonized/.

12. Dorothy Kim, "White Supremacists Have Weaponized an Imaginary Viking Past."

FURTHER READING

This list is limited to print scholarship and focuses on post-medieval misuses of the Middle Ages. In general, we list books and full journal issues rather than articles or chapters. For an interactive bibliography of digital writing on medievalism and additional resources, please see our website at *devilshistorians.com*.

Aberth, John. *Contesting the Middle Ages: Debates That Are Changing Our Narrative of Medieval History*. London: Routledge, 2019.

Alexander, Michael. *Medievalism: The Middle Ages in Modern England*. New Haven, CT: Yale University Press, 2007.

Albin, Andrew, Mary C. Erler, Thomas O'Donnell, Nicholas L. Paul, and Nina Rowe, eds. *Whose Middle Ages? Teachable Moments for an Ill-Used Past*. New York: Fordham University Press, 2019.

Altschul, Nadia, and Kathleen Davis. *Medievalisms in the Postcolonial World: The Idea of the "Middle Ages" Outside Europe*. Baltimore: Johns Hopkins University Press, 2010.

Arnold, Martin. *Thor: Myth to Marvel*. New York: Continuum, 2011.

Aronstein, Susan. *Hollywood Knights: Arthurian Cinema and the Politics of Nostalgia*. New York: Palgrave Macmillan, 2005.

Aronstein, Susan, and Tison Pugh, eds. *The Disney Middle Ages: A Fairy-Tale and Fantasy Past*. New York: Palgrave Macmillan, 2012.

Baker, Kelly J. *The Gospel According to the Klan: The KKK's Appeal to Protestant America, 1915–1930*. Lawrence: University Press of Kansas, 2011.

Barczewski, Stephanie. *Myth and National Identity in Nineteenth-Century Britain: The Legends of King Arthur and Robin Hood*. Oxford: Oxford University Press, 2000.

Bethencourt, Francisco. *Racisms: From the Crusades to the Twentieth Century*. Princeton, NJ: Princeton University Press, 2015.

Bryden, Inga. *Reinventing King Arthur: The Arthurian Legends in Victorian Culture*. London: Routledge, 2016.

Caputo, Nina, and Hannah Johnson, eds. "The Holocaust and the Middle Ages." *postmedieval* 5, no. 3 (Fall 2014).

Carroll, Shiloh. *Medievalism in* A Song of Ice and Fire *and* Game of Thrones. Cambridge: D.S. Brewer, 2018.

Chazan, Robert. *Medieval Stereotypes and Modern Antisemitism.* Berkeley: University of California Press, 1997.

D'Arcens, Louise, ed. *The Cambridge Companion to Medievalism.* Cambridge: Cambridge University Press, 2016.

D'Arcens, Louise, and Andrew Lynch. *International Medievalism and Popular Culture.* New York: Cambria, 2014.

Eco, Umberto. *Travels in Hyperreality.* London: Picador, 1987.

Elliott, Andrew B.R. *Medievalism, Politics, and Mass Media: Appropriating the Middle Ages in the Twenty-First Century.* Woodbridge, UK: D.S. Brewer, 2017.

———. *Remaking the Middle Ages: The Methods of Cinema and History in Portraying the Modern World.* Jefferson, NC: McFarland & Company, 2011.

Emery, Elizabeth, and Richard Utz, eds. *Medievalism: Key Critical Terms.* Cambridge: D.S. Brewer, 2014.

Finke, Laurie A., and Martin B. Shichtman. *Cinematic Illuminations: The Middle Ages on Film.* Baltimore: Johns Hopkins University Press, 2010.

———. *King Arthur and the Myth of History.* Gainesville: University Press of Florida, 2004.

Finn, Kavita Mudan, ed. *Fan Phenomena: Game of Thrones.* Chicago: University of Chicago Press, 2017.

Frankel, Valerie Estelle. *Women in* Game of Thrones: *Power, Conformity, and Resistance.* Jefferson, NC: McFarland, 2014.

Fugelso, Karl, ed. *Studies in Medievalism XXVIII: Medievalism and Discrimination.* Cambridge: D.S. Brewer, 2019.

Gabriele, Matthew, and Cord J. Whitaker, eds. "The Ghosts of the Nineteenth Century and the Future of Medieval Studies." *postmedieval* 10, no. 2 (June 2019).

Gardell, Mattias. *Gods of the Blood: The Pagan Revival and White Separatism.* Durham, NC: Duke University Press, 2003.

Harty, Kevin J. *The Reel Middle Ages: American, Western and Eastern European, Middle Eastern, and Asian Films about Medieval Europe.* Jefferson, NC: McFarland, 1999.

———, ed. *The Vikings on Film: Essays on Depictions of the Nordic Middle Ages.* Jefferson, NC: McFarland, 2011.

Haydock, Nickolas, and Ed Risden, eds. *Hollywood in the Holy Land: Essays on Film Depictions of the Crusades and Christian-Muslim Clashes.* Jefferson, NC: McFarland, 2009.

Holsinger, Bruce. *Neomedievalism, Neoconservatism, and the War on Terror*. Chicago: Prickly Paradigm Press, 2007.

Horswell, Mike. *The Rise and Fall of British Crusader Medievalism, c. 1825–1945*. New York: Routledge, 2018.

Kamenetsky, Christa. *Children's Literature in Hitler's Germany: The Cultural Policy of National Socialism*. Athens: Ohio University Press, 1984.

Kim, Dorothy. *Digital Whiteness and Medieval Studies*. York: Arc Humanities Press, 2019.

Larrington, Carolyne. *Winter Is Coming: The Medieval World of Game of Thrones*. London: I.B. Tauris, 2016.

Lipton, Sara. *Dark Mirror: The Medieval Origins of Anti-Jewish Iconography*. New York: Metropolitan Books, 2014.

Matthews, David. *Medievalism*. New York: Boydell and Brewer, 2015.

McArthur, Colin. *Brigadoon, Braveheart and the Scots: Distortions of Scotland in Hollywood Cinema*. London: I.B. Tauris, 2003.

Miller, Mary Dockray. *Public Medievalists, Racism, and Suffrage in the American Women's College*. New York: Palgrave Macmillan, 2017.

Montoya, Alicia C. *Medievalist Enlightenment from Charles Perrault to Jean-Jacques Rousseau*. Cambridge: D.S. Brewer, 2013.

Moreland, Kim Ileen. *The Medievalist Impulse in American Literature: Twain, Adams, Fitzgerald, and Hemingway*. Charlottesville: University of Virginia Press, 1996.

Paul, Nicholas, and Suzanne Yeager. *Remembering the Crusades: Myth, Image, and Identity*. Baltimore: Johns Hopkins University Press, 2012.

Phillips, Jonathan. *The Life and Legend of the Sultan Saladin*. New Haven, CT: Yale University Press, 2019.

Pugh, Tison. *Queer Chivalry: The Myth of White Masculinity in Southern Literature*. Charlottesville: University of Virginia Press, 2013.

Pugh, Tison, and Angela Jane Weisl. *Medievalisms: Making the Past in the Present*. London: Routledge, 2013.

Ramey, Lynn Tarte, and Tison Pugh, eds. *Race, Class, and Gender in "Medieval" Cinema*. New York: Palgrave Macmillan, 2007.

Simmons, Clare. *Popular Medievalism in Romantic-Era Britain*. New York: Palgrave Macmillan, 2016.

Snyder, Louis L. *The Roots of German Nationalism*. Ann Arbor, MI: UMI Books on Demand, 1997.

Sturtevant, Paul B. *The Middle Ages in Popular Imagination: Memory, Film, and Medievalism*. London: Bloomsbury Academic, 2018.

Toswell, M.J. *Today's Medieval University*. Kalamazoo, MI: Arc Humanities Press, 2017.

Utz, Richard. *Medievalism: A Manifesto*. Kalamazoo, MI: Arc Humanities Press, 2017.

Vernon, Matthew. *The Black Middle Ages: Race and the Construction of the Middle Ages*. New York: Palgrave Macmillan, 2018.

Warren, Michelle R. *Creole Medievalism: Colonial France and Joseph Bédier's Middle Ages*. Minneapolis: University of Minnesota Press, 2011.

Watson, Ritchie Devon, Jr. *Normans and Saxons: Southern Race Mythology and the Intellectual History of the American Civil War*. Baton Rouge: Louisiana State University Press, 2009.

Whitaker, Cord J. *Black Metaphors: Modern Racism/Medieval Race-Thinking*. Philadelphia: University of Pennsylvania Press, 2019.

Wollenberg, Daniel. *Medieval Imagery in Today's Politics*. Leeds: Arc Humanities Press, 2019.

Young, Helen. "'It's the Middle Ages, Yo!' Race, Neo/medievalisms, and the World of *Dragon Age*." *The Year's Work in Medievalism* 27 (2012): 2–9.

———. *Race and Popular Fantasy Literature: Habits of Whiteness*. New York: Routledge, 2016.

INDEX

Figures indicated by page numbers in italics

geographical determinism and,
99–100
medieval aristocracy and, 97–99
religious belief and, 100
See also white supremacy
Rai, Champat, 140
Rainey, Joseph, 83
Rambaran-Olm, Mary, 93
rape. *See* sexual assault and rape
culture
Raymond d'Aguilers, 74
Raziya (sultana of Delhi), 23
Reagan, Ronald, 43, 165n21
religion
diversity within, 20–21, 26–27,
146–47
gender identities and, 124–25
interfaith relations, 75–79
racism and, 100
science and, 147
sexuality and, 147–48
violence within, 79
women and, 23, 147
See also Christians; Jews;
Muslims
religious extremism, 127–49
Biblical Patriarchy movement,
129–32
fundamentalism as modern
phenomenon, 128–29
Hindu Nationalists, 140
ISIS, 127–28, 136–40
literalist movements, 128,
142–45
vs. medieval religious
experiences, 146–49
pagan movements, 140–42
in Roman Catholic Church,
132–36
Renaissance, 9, 11, 15–16, 21,
31, 79
Revels, Hiram Rhodes, 83
Richard Coer de Lyon (romance), 74
Robertson, Phil, 68

Robin Hood legend, 19, 21, 109
Roman Catholic Church
British cultural diversity and, 50
conversion via amalgamation, 32
extremism in modern, 132–36
political role, 30
witch trials and, 9
women and, 23, 147
See also Christians
romance (medieval genre), 97–98
The Romance of the Rose, 24
Roman Empire
amalgamation by, 31–32
conquest of Britain, 49
geographical determinism and, 99
Julian marriage laws, 1–2, 5
origin stories and nationalism,
3, 29, 30
Renaissance inspiration from,
11, 31
sexuality in, 121
Romantic Revival, 31–35
Der Ring des Nibelungen
(Wagner), 33–35, 48
Grimm Brothers and fairy tales,
32–33
inspiration from medieval
period, 31–32
Romney, Mitt, 49
Romulus and Remus, 3, 29
Roof, Dylann, 87
Russia, 23, 30, 41, 44–45, 69
Rykener, John, 24–25

S
Sacrobosco, Johannes de
De Sphaera Mundi, 16
Saladin, 62–64, 78
Salmon, Andy, 39
same-sex relationships, 24, 104,
122–23. *See also* LGBTQ+
people
Samuel HaNagid, 76
Santiago de Compostela, 26

Wilson, Randy, 131
Winter, Evan
  Rage of Dragons, 158
witch trials, 9–10, 147, 161n2
  (ch. 1)
Withers, Linette, 155–56
Wolfram von Eschenbach
  Parzival, 96, 100
Wollenberg, Daniel, 93
Wolves of Vinland, 88, 141
women. *See* gender and
  sexuality
Wood, Graeme, 128

X
xenophobia, 14–15, 44–45, 53–54,
  70, 88–89
Xue Tao, 117

Y
Yde et Olive (chivalric story), 25
Yiddish, 142
Young, Helen, 93, 157
Yu Xuanji, 117

Z
Zarquali, al-, 147